FIRES, FLOODS, AND TAXICABS

JEFFREY D. ROTH

FIRES, FLOODS, AND TAXICABS

TAKING A BITE OUT OF BIG APPLE BUREAUCRACY

LIONCREST
PUBLISHING

FIRES, FLOODS, AND TAXICABS

Taking a Bite Out of Big Apple Bureaucracy

ISBN   978-1-5445-1879-4 *Hardcover*

978-1-5445-1878-7 *Paperback*

978-1-5445-1877-0 *Ebook*

For the doers who choose to serve the public. Yours is a special calling. Our institutions need you now, perhaps more than ever.

CONTENTS

INTRODUCTION

"Two Firefighters Are Dead in Deutsche Bank Fire," read the headline following the tragic fire at Ground Zero (Rivera and Santos 2007). Less than ninety days into my position in city government, I was assigned to review the interagency operations of the principal city departments responsible for regulating the teardown of the Deutsche Bank Building, which had been damaged beyond repair in the World Trade Center attacks. Something had gone wrong during the teardown, and a fire had broken out, leading to the death of two firefighters. A city demanded answers.

"This cannot happen again," said my boss. That was the start of my nearly fifteen years in NYC government, during which I worked on some of the toughest, most complex issues. It was everything I wanted: the chance to have an impact and make real, positive change in my city. I was fresh out of graduate school and excited to apply my skills to public policy, but I soon ran into a formidable foe: bureaucracy.

Change is difficult...

That's where you are: stepping into the fray for the first time. You are just starting to experience the romance of government—running across the street with printed presentations under your arm for a meeting with city hall decision makers or to appear before a city council hearing. You are part of an engine that impacts people's lives. But perhaps you're also experiencing your first pangs of disillusionment as well.

You probably came to the public sector because you are different from most people you know. You are driven by the need to make a difference, to leave the world a little better than you found it, to tackle complex problems and find ways to improve the lives of people who live in your neighborhood and community. Whether you are passionate about social justice, equality, and fairness, or you're the type of person who sits at the Department of Motor Vehicles and thinks of thousands of ways to improve the experience, government is where you can make changes.

Change will not come easily. You will step in and have

to roll up your sleeves. You will get dirty, for sure, and maybe even a little bloody along the way. That is to be expected when you are hell-bent on making an organization better, different, more transparent, more efficient, or fairer. You will require brute force and a willingness to be flexible as you uncover the intricacies of the machinery of government.

Perhaps you have recently been handed a project or been asked to deliver for your boss, and the problem seems too big, even overwhelming. Perhaps you have tried a few things only to find that the bureaucratic resistance to change is too great, so you feel beaten down. I know that feeling—I've been there—but we need you! Our civic institutions require people like you who are willing to do the hard work of making things a little better. Don't give up.

...but possible.

A career in the public sector is challenging, but you *can* make a difference—and it's worth it when you do.

Over my career, I learned to navigate my way through the maze of bureaucratic inertia. Bureaucracy is no easy foe, and I relied on my incredible teams to make changes. Being part of those teams and the government in the United States' largest city, at the center of the world, was intoxicating. Working on matters such as flood mitigation, fire, taxi data, and technology innovation, I applied ingenuity in my quest to get things done against the odds. What made it so exciting? As NYC government goes, so goes the world. It was a chance to lead in creating change and making government smarter, more responsive, and more accessible to the millions of people who call NYC home.

During my time in NYC government, I've had the privilege of seeing several of my major career milestones and accomplishments marked in newspaper headlines.

A *Wall Street Journal* article headlined "How New York's Fire Department Uses Data Mining" drew attention to our work. "New York City has about a million buildings, and each year 3,000 of them erupt in a major fire. Can officials predict which ones will go up in flames?" (Dwoskin 2014). We certainly thought so, and we built a team of data-smart analysts to find ways to do it. "Think *Moneyball* for firefighting," offered one article about the project (McEnery 2014).

The headline "Uber Has a Clever Response to a Proposed Law that Could Kneecap the Company in One of Its Largest Markets" came at the height of a battle between NYC and Uber, when the city had found its footing in regulating the megacompany and its saturation of NYC's for-hire vehicle market (Kosoff 2015). The Taxi and Limousine Commission (TLC) determined methods for controlling the ride-hailing app companies, but it was a bloody battle against the anti-regulatory, billion-dollar behemoths, one among many political clashes involving the TLC that I would find myself caught in the middle of another five years later.

"After Long Process, City Launches New Department of Veterans' Services" heralded the establishment of the first new NYC agency since the late 1990s, when the city had created the Office of Emergency Management (Pazmino 2016). Building a government startup was among the most challenging endeavors I have ever faced. In a monumental effort against structural inertia, we built a new agency from the ground up that was dedicated to supporting veterans.

Through it all, one thing missing from my desktop was a guidebook to help me navigate the difficulties and challenges I encountered as an urban analyst. Everything from interagency coordination and process redesign to building a brand-new city agency, leading teams, and being grilled by the city council had to be learned along the way, but I worked with brilliant people who inspired me and taught me how to get things done.

THE GUIDEBOOK I ALWAYS WANTED

With this book, I have created the guidebook that I wish

I had when I started my career. I take you through some of the memorable projects, programs, and initiatives in which I took part in city government and explain what I learned along the way. I start with a roadmap for getting things done. The first part of the book helps you define a start point and end point and chart a path from where you are to where you want to go. This approach is particularly helpful when you are handed a nebulous or ill-defined problem. Many of the problems I faced required research, understanding, and description, and all of them needed a definition of what we were trying to solve. They all needed a path to the solution as well as tools and techniques to maintain the project's scope and keep it safe from derailment.

In the second part of the book, I delve into some specific situations you're likely to face in your career, from building teams to managing emergencies. I offer insights into the hard lessons I learned as I helped build new teams and an agency in the context of city government. I share how, when I stepped into the political arena, I got knocked down in a tough lesson in NYC politics.

I offer these lessons and insights as a guide, something you can reference along the way. When you need a fresh perspective or a new idea, delve into these pages. You will learn about analyzing problems, testing solutions, interviewing people, conducting ride-alongs, and so much more. I invite you to come along with me as I fought in the trenches to solve a host of issues and problems. I collected tools, techniques, and lessons along the way, and here I share the ones I found to be the most reliable, the things I kept in my toolkit, so that when I didn't know exactly what to do, I could turn to them and navigate my way to the next step.

This book is for you if you need a boost in the incredibly difficult work of supporting decision makers and governing. Read it. Learn from it. Share what you learn and share the change that you lead. And please, please, please, keep going! We need you.

PART I

A PROCESS ROADMAP

"There are four steps to land navigation. Being given an objective and the requirement to move there, you must know where you are, plan the route, stay on the route, and recognize the objective."

—MAP READING AND LAND NAVIGATION, US ARMY

CHAPTER 1

KNOW WHERE YOU ARE

When you are confronted with a project, initiative, or objective and don't know where to start, start by painting the picture.

"If you define the problem correctly, you almost have the solution."

—STEVE JOBS

It was eighty-three degrees in the city that day. The sun was shining, and lower Manhattan was abuzz with the sounds of demolition and construction. At 3:37 p.m., a citizen called 911 to report a fire on a scaffolding at a building near Rector Street, one block from the World Trade Center site. The NYC Fire Department (FDNY) sounded an alarm two seconds later to dispatch two engines, two ladders, and a battalion chief. Additional calls poured in, all reporting a fire at the vacant thirty-eight-story Deutsche Bank Building at 130 Liberty Street, which was undergoing abatement of hazardous materials and demolition due to the damage caused when the south tower of the World Trade Center collapsed onto it on September 11, 2001.

At 3:40 p.m., the responding units sent a 10-75 radio code, or "All Hands," signifying that all the personnel from the responding units were engaged in fighting the fire. In other words, it was a serious fire and more resources were needed. Over the next hour, additional alarms were sounded to activate more emergency personnel. Hundreds arrived on the scene to battle the blaze, which was not behaving as most high-rise fires would. Something different was happening here.

At 4:38 p.m., a roll call was conducted by fire department personnel for the fire floors fifteen through seventeen. Some firefighters did not respond, so a Mayday was sounded for the missing members. This happened while crews stretched a hose line up the side of the building to get water on the fire, which was necessary because of an inoperable standpipe.

The inside of the building presented a maze, as each floor had been partitioned into asbestos and hazardous material containment areas for the abatement process, with temporary walls constructed to trap hazardous materials during the cleanup. These partitions blocked egress and stairwells. Negative air pressure ventilation systems designed to keep hazardous materials inside the building changed the behavior of the smoke and fire (Kugler 2007). The smoke was not rising into the air (as is typical of a high-rise fire) but was sucked back into the building. The negative pressure also changed the behavior of the fire, pulling it inward and forcing it downward from the fire floors to lower floors.

The building had been under floor-by-floor demolition while abatement was done simultaneously. The crews would conduct the hazardous material abatement on one floor, and when they finished, they'd move to the next floor down while a demolition crew worked on the floor just vacated. The standpipe and sprinkler system were inoperable as a result of the teardown.

The entire project to take down the Deutsche Bank Building had been filed under a series of alteration permits (NYC Fire Wire 2016) that regulated partial demolition practices for dismantling "structural members, floors, interior bearing walls, and/or exterior walls or portions thereof." The project was not filed as a full building demolition, which would have been treated differently and was defined as the "dismantling, razing, or removal of all of a building or structure" (City of New York 2008).

At 5:20 p.m. that day, two firefighters were found uncon-scious and transported to an area hospital. At 5:36 p.m., a third member was found and also transported to the hospital. Less than half an hour later, two of the mem-bers experienced full cardiac arrest; firefighters Robert Beddia and Joseph Graffagnino tragically gave their lives in battling the fire.

The tower continued to burn for seven hours before fire-fighters finally extinguished the flames. Black smoke had pumped into the air from this sacred spot near Ground Zero in lower Manhattan. The death of two firefighters demanded answers, and the city needed to understand how a fire of this magnitude had occurred and killed two of NYC's bravest. Mayor Bloomberg called the incident "another cruel blow to our city and to the Fire Department" (Rivera and Santos 2007), alluding to the FDNY's losing so many (343, to be precise) only six years earlier at the World Trade Center.

A few days after the fire, my boss told me I needed to understand the process of building demolition in NYC. This was my first job in NYC government, in the Mayor's Office of Operations where I worked as a policy analyst at the end of Mayor Bloomberg's second term. Diving right into this experience was my only option because, as the new guy, I didn't know much of anything. I had few rela-tionships in city government at the time, but I dived in with a curious mindset and started to paint a picture of the situation with tools I knew would help me.

START WITH CURIOSITY

The first step in any project is to be curious and dive in. Strip away what you *think* you know and start asking questions. I always relished figuring out how things worked (or didn't work as the case may be), and you should enjoy the process of digging into an operation and learning how people do their jobs.

In this case, city hall had enlisted our team's help in understanding the information flow among the principal city agencies that had a regulatory role in the teardown of buildings. Our team, the Project Management Group at the Mayor's Office of Operations, was essentially a group of in-house consultants who were tasked with large-scale, interagency projects of mayoral priority. We excelled at dissecting complex projects into actionable steps and understanding the nuts-and-bolts processes that made the city's vast government hum.

Being curious and knowing little about this specific problem set allowed me to ask questions from a fresh perspective with absolutely no baseline assumptions or inaccurate perceptions.

The main question from my perspective was why no one

had fully understood what was going on inside this building when three key city agencies played a regulatory role in its razing.

WHAT GOES ON INSIDE THE BLACK BOX?

We convened an interagency task force to kick off the work about to take place. Representatives of several city agencies would gather to discuss how the city was going to ensure that the problems that led to the deaths of two firefighters would be fixed and never allowed to happen again.

A day or two later, I sat in the conference room for our kickoff meeting at 253 Broadway, directly across the street from city hall. The leaders of the three principal agencies had gathered to discuss the scale and scope of our project, and my boss laid out how we would delve into their operations and processes to understand what had happened. We packed in around the long table in the windowless room. Pens and notebooks rested on the table as my boss laid out our approach, commanding the room from one end of the table. That's when a senior chief from the FDNY leaned forward and offered the following succinct statement: "None of this would have happened if we knew what goes on inside that black box."

To abate the hazardous materials, the crews had built containment areas or structures that kept the hazardous materials from escaping into the air. These structures, combined with negative air pressure machines, kept the asbestos and debris inside the building as cleanup crews in hazmat suits and ventilators removed all the particles. The problem was that the building's containment areas were built in ways that blocked exits, stairwells, hallways, and doorways (Baker 2008). A firefighter crawling on the floor with zero visibility faced a very hard time in navigating that labyrinth of structures and machinery.

This is what the chief was talking about. These containment areas were in effect mazes, and the FDNY had little knowledge of what was inside them. Why? Because the city's Department of Environmental Protection (DEP), not the FDNY, regulated hazardous material abatement and how it was performed. And who oversaw the teardown of the building itself? The Department of Buildings (DOB). Meanwhile, the FDNY was responsible for overseeing the building inspections that ensured that no life-threatening safety issues were present in the case of an emergency, such as a fire. All told, this was a complicated, interconnected web of activities and regulations with no central authority overseeing all the components to ensure that each stakeholder had a complete picture of what was happening inside that building.

On the day I joined the chief, my boss, others from the city agencies, and members of the mayor's staff from city hall, I had been in my role for less than three months and had only recently set foot in NYC for the first time to start my job in the Mayor's Office of Operations. Just prior, I had completed studies for my master's degree and, for a summer, had been an intern for James J. Fiorentini, the mayor of Haverhill, Massachusetts. I knew from those experiences that city government, at any scale, was complicated and required a great deal of cross-collaboration and coordination. In my limited experience, I had seen how we managed to get a boardwalk project back on track by convening a meeting of all the stakeholders. The project, which had been stalled for years, was on hold because all the parties involved were pointing at one another and claiming that they were waiting for decisions or for this or that piece of information, even though they were all committed to completing the project itself. It reminded me of the scarecrow from *The Wizard of Oz*, pointing in two directions at once. In the case in NYC, I was not an expert who could provide insight into the complicated regulatory issues, but I knew my boss expected me to understand those processes and identify the issues that had led to those complications.

I needed a better understanding of our current status: the existing systems, people, and processes that had contributed to this situation. Had the FDNY known about the activities within the containment areas? Had the DOB ensured that the containment areas complied with the building code? Had the DEP surveyed the sites prior to this happening? I had a million questions as I determined how to proceed.

KNOW WHERE YOU ARE

One of the main things I learned from this experience was that in order to change policy, you have to know not only your destination (although that is certainly necessary) but also where you are. Only by understanding the starting point can you begin charting a path to your desired end point.

End points, I have found, are the easier ones to identify. A leader commits to a bold vision, as in President Kennedy's famous speech proposing that the United States send a man to the moon and return him safely to Earth before the end of the 1960s. The end point? To the moon and back safely. But what about the starting point?

Often, the harder part is defining the current reality—the start point. Many times throughout my career, I have seen project teams jump in without establishing a problem statement to define where they are. At best, part of the problem gets fixed. Maybe. At worst, resources, time, and money are invested in fixing a nonexistent problem.

In this instance, our team was able to paint a picture of the existing reality, which highlighted areas needing change. It was a lot of work and required painstaking research, collaboration, interviews, and staff time. No binder on a shelf offered a blueprint for how everything worked in government, and we had no simple map or how-to guide. What we had was a three-part strategy: collect, organize, and assess.

COLLECT

The best way to start? Get the on-the-ground truth. Collect as much on-the-ground data as you can, and if you cannot, ask others on the team to do it. Nothing offers more clarity than spending time with people doing the job and getting a firsthand sense of how things happen. This will either clarify things you were uncertain about or will highlight things that need changing that you had not even thought about.

During this project, we toured high-rise construction and demolition sites and learned how site safety was conducted. We joined DOB personnel as they inspected buildings for key safety concerns, and we rode along with FDNY fire units to understand the life and fire safety issues they looked for when inspecting buildings under construction or demolition. We also toured the DEP to understand how abatement inspections occurred. All these tours, interviews, and surveys gave us invaluable information on how things were done.

Starting with a concept on paper and then seeing it on the ground switched on a number of light bulbs and improved our understanding of the overall process. It also allowed us to ask questions of the people who actually did the work (to avoid getting answers that were filtered and potentially skewed by traveling through multiple layers of management). This created opportunities to engage with people who knew how the processes worked and could show me the systems they used, how they tracked information, and what resources would make their jobs better. Many of the ideas that emerged in this report and others were directly attributable to the good people who were doing the work every day.

Many tools and techniques are needed to gather this kind of on-the-ground data. The ones I've found most critical are interviews, ride-alongs, mystery shopping, surveys, and focus groups. These tools are helpful in almost any situation, and all of them will give you a deeper sense of where you are.

INTERVIEWS

Conducting interviews of key stakeholders and the people doing the work is fundamental to any project. They can be done one-on-one, in group settings, in focus groups, or in small huddles—anything that allows you to elicit information from a team. This is crucial for any project and is often where a nebulous project will begin to take form.

Listen to those who do the work. Ask for their opinions, perspectives, and where they believe change is necessary. If you do enough of these, the problem statement will often write itself. Do not be afraid to follow up and ask for the interviewee's perspective and opinion along the way. Keep meticulous notes and write a detailed summary of each of your interviews, which allows you to review them periodically to look for insights you may have missed, recognize places where you need more detail or insight, and find the emerging patterns.

SAMPLE QUESTIONS FOR STAKEHOLDER INTERVIEWS

Understanding the Process, Roles, and Responsibilities of Staff

- Describe your typical day. Walk me through a typical shift.
- Tell me more about that.
- What exactly does that mean?
- Help me understand.
- Describe how your typical day changes. What causes it to change?
- What is your role?
- Who do you work with?
- Who do you report to?
- What are you responsible for at the beginning of your shift and at the end of your shift?

- What tools does the organization provide? How well do they work?
- What tools would help you do your job better?

Understanding Systems, Data, and Tools

- What data tools do you use during the day?
- How well do they perform their intended functions?
- Are there things happening during your day or in your work processes that the organization should capture or better understand?
- How do you define a particular data element (e.g., response times)? Knowing how a user defines particular data can clarify where systems collect data that may not be fully understood.

Understanding Where Change Is Necessary

- What is the best part of your job?
- What is the worst part of your job?
- What about your day is most frustrating?
- What is the hardest part of your job?
- If you could wave a magic wand, what would you do to make this job easier? Better? Smarter? More streamlined?
- What tools or systems would help?
- What problems or issues do you see that have gone unaddressed? Why haven't they been solved?
- How could the organization save money in this specific task, function, or process?

Other Items

- Who else should I speak to?
- Who is the contact for X function?
- Do you have contact information for them that you can share with me?

Of these questions, one of my favorites is, "If you could wave a magic wand…" Another way to ask this question is, "If you could have anything, what would it be?" "Magic" questions like this allow people to offer thinking that is not constrained by limits. Of course, you cannot provide everything they desire, but you may find patterns or commonalities that are mentioned over and over again by different people that could improve an operation or the unit's ability to complete a task. Look for these patterns and find ways to improve them.

RIDE-ALONGS

Ride-alongs are a must. Ride-alongs are active interviews, a chance for you to go out and experience a situation with key stakeholders. During the research of the Deutsche Bank Building fire, our team joined multiple ride-alongs with city employees responsible for conducting inspections of buildings undergoing construction, demolition, or abatement. What I learned in this process was how city inspectors approach a construction and demolition site, what they are looking for, how to spot the telltale signs of negligence at a construction site, and how site safety is actually implemented. We learned how to trace a standpipe and how to read the valves to ensure the pressure was correct. We learned where building floor plans and site safety plans are kept on file with the building manager. And we learned the key items each particular agency was looking for when they inspected a building.

I learned how complicated all this is by spending time with crews who did that very work, who explained to me in detail how they spent their day and the challenges they faced. These things are absolutely critical to any project and to being a well-informed and experienced project manager or policy analyst. I have seen my own new hires holding their own against veteran city managers because they had conducted ride-alongs and had firsthand experience of how things actually worked. These are musts! Ride-alongs should be done regularly, not only in the information collection stage but even in the maintenance stage of a project or program.

MYSTERY SHOPPING

Mystery shopping means conducting secret visits or calls to your customer-facing teams to see how they handle a process. That is, pretend to be a customer calling or stopping at a location with a particular concern and see how your team handles it. Mystery shopping can and should be done throughout a project's life to ensure that your tasks are making the progress you desire.

In NYC, the government is big enough that being recognized is unlikely. If anonymity is a concern (e.g., in a smaller municipality where everyone knows your name and walking in would probably add no mystery to the shopping), consider having interns or temporary employees conduct these visits and provide assessments of their experience.

Mystery shopping and calling soon give you a picture of the current reality as well as a sense of the customer's experience when interacting with your organization.

SURVEYS

Surveys are an easy, low-cost method of obtaining more information about the current situation affecting a group or constituency. Multiple online solutions allow for seamless integration with client relationship managers, and email solutions can collect responses from literally hundreds of respondents or more. I have used these successfully in all my projects. You can survey the public at large for input on a particular policy question. You can survey your stakeholders for greater clarity on how to improve a program or project, and you can use surveys to better understand the elements of your target demographic or constituency. In NYC government, I have seen surveys used to size up situations and to collect information about policy questions and employees' skillsets and computer systems used to enable various functions. Simple, low-cost tools make this quick and easy.

FOCUS GROUPS

Convene groups of constituents or stakeholders who may be affected by a particular policy or initiative to solicit their feedback and insights on how a particular problem can be addressed. Right away, you will hear the essence of the problem from those grappling with it in their daily lives. If you plan to conduct quantitative research, make sure your groups comprise diverse segments of your target population and are statistically representative.

ORGANIZE

Once you've collected the relevant data, you need to organize it in order to make sense of it. Process flow diagrams are your greatest tool at this stage of the process.

Throughout our information-gathering stage for the Deutsche Bank fire investigation, we took meticulous notes and pieced together all the information from various sources. From this, we created process diagrams every day, making updates as we collected a new bit of information here or a new insight there.

The diagrams allowed me to step back from the process, so to speak, and view it from a different angle. Sometimes, stepping back from a situation and allowing it to marinate creates clarity or identifies places where information is puzzling or confusing. Discovering where the picture was still hazy allowed us to return to our stakeholders for further clarification. If a process was hazy to our understanding, it almost always required an improvement because if it was hard for the stakeholders to explain, the process was more than likely convoluted and merited being streamlined or changed.

PROCESS FLOW DIAGRAMS IN ACTION

For this project, I decided to start by interviewing personnel from the DOB. As the agency responsible for permitting the teardown of buildings in NYC, it would help me understand the overall process. Once I better understood how buildings were torn down, I could plug the role of the DEP and FDNY into that. I set up a meeting with the DOB's operations team, who came to our office to explain how it all worked.

Prior to their arrival, I listed my questions about tearing down buildings. How does a building owner get a permit to do that? What rules do they have to follow? So on and so forth.

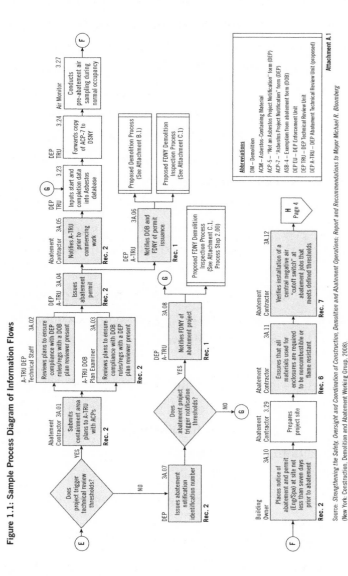

Figure 1.1: Sample Process Diagram of Information Flows

Source: *Strengthening the Safety, Oversight and Coordination of Construction, Demolition and Abatement Operations: Report and Recommendations to Mayor Michael R. Bloomberg* (New York: Construction, Demolition and Abatement Working Group, 2008).

Attachment A.1

Abbreviations

DM – Demolition
ACM – Asbestos-Containing Material
ACP-5 – "Not an Asbestos Project Notification" form (DEP)
ACP-7 – "Asbestos Project Notification" form (DOB)
ASB-4 – Exemption from abatement form (DOB)
DEP EU – DEP Enforcement Unit
DEP TRU – DEP Technical Review Unit
DEP A-TRU – DEP Abatement Technical Review Unit (proposed)

Per our team's standard, I would create process flow diagrams of all the activities that occurred to develop a complete understanding of the situation. Process flow diagrams, aka flowcharts, are a graphic representation of the sequential steps in a business process. In my army training, I had learned to be comfortable with not knowing how a situation worked and to ask a lot of questions—even seemingly elementary questions—to ensure I completely understood a situation. I walked to the copy machine and pulled out a stack of tabloid-size paper that would come in handy for sketching out the process diagrams. I sharpened a few pencils and set up the conference room table to meet the team from the DOB. Three gentlemen arrived, and after a quick round of introductions, we sat down and got on with business.

"OK, so I need to understand how buildings are demolished in New York City," I said as I prepared to sketch. I looked up at the team leader. His eyes were as big as saucers.

"Jeff, that's impossible to fully explain. There are literally hundreds of permutations that can occur depending on the building and what they are trying to do. Is this a full demolition? Is this a partial?"

I paused for a minute, having a limited understanding of the terms.

"Let's keep it high level; maybe you can just help me understand the common steps a building owner goes through," I suggested.

The team leader laughed and leaned back in his chair, convinced that my efforts would be futile. We started anyway. He began to explain the process, and I drew a little box in the upper left-hand corner of the page.

"Building owner submits an application to conduct demolition," it said. I then asked what happened next. The team looked at each other and began to discuss the steps to sound it out.

"Well, before they can proceed, they have to be cleared for asbestos abatement," they offered.

This was the exact process that the Deutsche Bank Building was undergoing in its hazardous materials abatement.

"Great," I said, drawing a diamond on the page that represented a decision point where the flow would split depending on asbestos abatement (yes or no).

"If the asbestos is abated," they continued, "they receive their initial permit. If it isn't, they must first complete the abatement process."

"OK, so if my abatement is complete, I tell DOB I'm complete?" There was silence. There had to be some method of notification when the abatement process was complete. They looked at each other.

"Well, that's DEP. They certify completion of the abatement."

"Right," I replied, "but how does DOB know when it has been abated?"

There was no easy answer to that question, and it transpired that this would be one of the crucial findings of the project. Nothing linked the DEP's certification that the abatement was complete to the building's proceeding with demolition. Three little boxes sketched on a page illuminated serious issues in the process and would ultimately lead to several significant recommendations and a reengineering of the process for information sharing between the DOB and the DEP.

The work continued as we painted a picture of the process, highlighting inconsistencies and areas for improvement along the way. The process flows were not completed in one meeting or two but in dozens of meetings and interviews with people who conducted the work at all three agencies. This involved drafting diagrams, receiving feedback in painstaking detail, and bringing the stakeholders to the table to agree that we had correctly captured the existing processes.

We went through dozens of versions of the process as we created and refined the diagrams, adding layers of detail about how things currently worked. We started the process diagraming with a broad understanding of how a building is demolished in NYC. The DOB had principal oversight of the regulations of that process, but the DEP and the FDNY had roles that plugged into that baseline process. I found that starting with a single, central process and defining it and the points where other entities plugged in enabled us to create a main focus. In this case, the teardown of a building was the central element, and the process started there, but hazardous material abatement played a key role and occurred simultaneously with the teardown of the Deutsche Bank Building.

ASSESS

As you form your picture, you want to continually assess and refine it. To ensure you don't get stuck in one point of view, create a way to step back from the situation and view it from different angles.

Many project teams create a situation room in which they put all the pieces together on the walls and move them around as their understanding changes. Find a way to use visuals to help you see the process unfold, envision the project's goals, or brainstorm, as in those TV whodunits on which gumshoes pin people and supporting evidence on corkboards to discover some new tidbit. I love this technique. If you have no board, sketch notes on chart paper or use a digital tool, anything that will let you step back and see the back-end processes so your brain can contemplate the problem or issue and provide solutions or new approaches. Listen to yourself. Where are you confused or unclear about something? Lean into that. Dig in. Ask more questions. Let people know what is hazy to you and try to get a clearer understanding. It will come, or if not, others are probably grappling with the same issue, so you can add it to your list of improvement areas!

Another technique I love is a *sticky notes explosion*. You can use this exercise to identify areas of improvement for a specific task or to overcome a project's inertia when it feels stalled. Often, when a team is struggling with how to improve and move toward a goal, I have them all brainstorm for five minutes (you don't need more time) with a stack of sticky notes in front of them. Put a question on the board, such as, "What can we do more of or less of as a team to improve [fill in the blank]." Set a timer and have each member of the team write down a thought, idea, frustration, pain point, or whatever comes to mind (it can even be a single word) to describe the situation. Each sticky note, however, can hold only one idea.

At the end of the five-minute brainstorm, ask for a volunteer to share a sticky note and place it on the wall, a whiteboard, or an empty table—someplace where everyone can see it. After the person sticks it there, other team members who have something similar or related place their sticky notes around it. Do this with a team, and you will find that dozens of ideas emerge that can all be grouped into a few (three to five) broad categories and perhaps a few subcategories. And voilà! You have action steps that help you understand where you are and what needs to be fixed. You will be amazed at what comes out of this simple yet very powerful exercise, which essentially discovers group consciousness.

MAKING AN IMPACT

In the Deutsche Bank fire project, once the baseline process was well defined, we reversed course and built in the process for abatement, coordinating with the DEP to understand how that process worked. After creating a draft, we identified the intersections between the DEP and the DOB where improvements could be made in how information was shared between agencies or where new touch points were required to provide more information or details that would help the DOB to understand what was being abated and how and whether the job was completed to standard.

Every change and new detail required an additional level of validation by each of the agencies, leading to some level of discussion and clarification. However, one beneficial outcome of this process was that it opened lines of communication between the agencies, which was ultimately one of the goals of the overall project.

In this case, we recommended enhancements to how the city regulated hazardous material abatement through the creation of an Abatement Technical Review Unit at the DEP. The central question about what was happening in the abatement containment areas, which had created a maze of partitions and blocked egresses, could be addressed by giving the DOB and the FDNY insight into what was happening inside those black boxes, just as the fire chief had so clearly articulated at the beginning of our research (City of New York 2008). Our goal was to ensure that no firefighter would enter into a dangerous situation like this again without the insight of what was happening inside. That by opening the lid on those black boxes and creating shared understanding between these key city agencies, we would save lives.

KEY TAKEAWAYS

Before you dive into where you want to go, paint a picture of where you are. In the Deutsche Bank fire investigation, painting the picture helped us define what and where the problems were. We first used all the tools to collect information—interviews, ride-alongs, surveys, and everything in between—to hone in on the pain points and size up the situation more accurately, and then we worked with the project team to organize our notes by creating detailed process diagrams and highlighting problems or potential issues. We could then assess the problem by determining whether we faced information or data-exchange issues, whether training or other resources were needed, or if changes were needed in local legislation or regulation.

A number of methods can define the starting point in a project or initiative; the important thing is taking the time to do it. Also, it is never too early. These tools work as readily at the commencement of a project as when you need a fresh perspective. In fact, for longer-term projects, practicing some of these methods to monitor and evaluate the overall project is a good idea.

Once you've identified your starting point, you can then move on to determining your specific objectives.

CHAPTER 2

DEFINE WHERE YOU WANT TO GO

When you need help identifying the objective, get elbows deep in the data.

"The greatest value of a picture is when it forces us to notice what we never expected to see."

—JOHN TUKEY

It was late summer 2008, and I was working with staff from the NYC Department of Environmental Protection (DEP). Someone handed me a map of citizen calls to 311 that reported street flooding and sewer backups during recent significant rain events. The page showed an outline of all five of NYC's boroughs with thousands of tiny dots stacked on top of one another, each representing a single call to 311 during the storms.

"Any thoughts on which neighborhoods were hardest hit?" I asked, trying to determine where the call volumes were heaviest. This was a couple of days after heavy storms had whipped through the city, tearing apart roofs, uprooting trees, and dumping so much rain that the city's wastewater system could not handle the flow. It started in the early morning hours of August 8, and it was determined that for the first time in recorded history, a tornado had touched down in Brooklyn, devastating several neighborhoods.

Other significant rain events had occurred that summer. Climate change had increased the amount and frequency of rain falling on the city, and city officials were developing a plan to protect people and property from future events. I joined a task force with others from the mayor's office, the DEP, the Department of Parks and Recreation, the Department of Buildings (DOB), and the Department of Transportation (DOT). The city's overall objective was clear—protect people and property from future flooding—but we didn't yet know what that would look like. We needed to better define where we wanted to go and identify the specific actions the city could take to achieve the overall goal. That's where my team came in. Our job was to identify hot spots across the city that seemed hardest hit by floodwaters, so that the city knew where and how to focus resources. Data would be the key to pinpointing those hot spots and identifying the actions the city needed to take.

DATA IS THE LIFEBLOOD OF PROJECT MANAGEMENT

NYC is a living laboratory. As a city with nearly nine million people that swells by another three million each day as commuters meander through tunnels and over bridges to enter it, NYC has data. Tons of data. In my time as a policy analyst, having the ability to build and deploy data analysis tools that were operationalized in real time across a city the size of New York was absolutely incredible.

During any year, NYC residents and visitors interact millions upon millions of times with city government. Using 311, the city's nonemergency call center, we can learn a tremendous amount about the city, its people, and their behavior. We also can use the data to understand the public's demand for services. For example, in calendar year 2018, the city had over twenty million calls to the 311 system (City of New York 2020).

During the city's 2018 fiscal year,[1] among the things the city experienced were over one million taxi or for-hire vehicle (Uber, Lyft, Gett, Via, etc.) trips per day; 1.5 million visits to the NYC online business portal; 259,584 crime-in-progress calls; 27,280 structural fires with an average 4:58 response time; 97 civilian fire fatalities; 568,737 life-threatening medical emergency incidents with an average 6:55 response time; 21,286 Community Emergency Response Team volunteer hours; 9,000 new

---

1   NYC's fiscal year is from July 1 to June 30.

construction starts; 3,193,000 tons of refuse; 3,202,200 total recreation center visits; 1,953 new HIV diagnoses; and 7,531 veterans and families engaged by the Department of Veterans' Services, with 2,791 veterans and their families receiving assistance.

All of these interactions, service requests, citizen complaints, and so on fill the city's data coffers with billions of records. For the policy nerd who wants to delve into the nuts and bolts of how a municipal government functions—or doesn't function as the case may be—no place rivals NYC with its mountains of information ripe for analysis, study, and insight. During my dozen years-plus in city government, data were at the epicenter of everything from understanding emergency incident response times to determining how the city could better serve its citizens. Data were foundational to identifying where policy interventions were needed to improve citizens' everyday lives.

Leveraging data to make decisions is not new, but at the time of the flooding project, NYC had experienced a convergence of leadership, data availability, and data infrastructure that enabled greater data and information sharing between city agencies. This allowed users to plug in and understand the city and its operations at an ever-deeper level.

DATA MATURITY: BUILD A FOUNDATION, THEN REFINE

In collecting data, you must understand that there is a hierarchy of data analysis. The foundation must be laid before moving up the scale to more sophisticated levels of data analysis and science.

I often refer to Davenport and Harris's (2017) analytical spectrum. This model displays the relationship between degree of difficulty of a specific type of data analysis (x-axis) and the value it brings to an organization (y-axis). For example, the question, "What happened?" can be answered by creating standard reports that provide descriptive statistics. These are fairly simple products to create, and although they have value, it is relatively low compared to more sophisticated forms of data intelligence. However, standard reports are absolutely foundational before reaching for the next level of data maturity. As the organization builds analytical capability, it can begin to answer more difficult questions such as, "What exactly is the problem?" "Why is this happening?" or "What if these trends continue?"—each requiring higher degrees of data analysis to answer. Ultimately, an organization strives to answer, "What will happen next?" and "What's the best that can happen?" as is the case with predictive analytics and resource optimization, highly sophisticated levels of data intelligence that add significant value to an organization.

Figure 2.1: Davenport and Harris's Analytical Spectrum

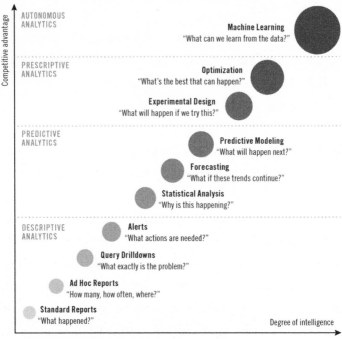

Assess where your team, unit, or organization is and first establish maturity at one layer before moving upward. If you lack simple reports and cannot promptly support ad hoc data requests, it is not the time to move toward predictive analytics. Build the foundation first, then proceed to answer the next set of questions.

Accordingly, with the flooding project, we started at the bottom of the data hierarchy with the raw data from 311 calls, each call represented by a dot on a map of NYC, before working our way up.

IDENTIFY POTENTIAL BLIND SPOTS

As you move up the data hierarchy, you must continually question exactly what the data points tell you and what they don't, searching for potential blind spots. Data is an incredibly powerful tool, but it doesn't always tell the full story.

For instance, on this project, 311 call data were instrumental in identifying the areas with significant issues. However, we recognized that the data were a measure of neighborhoods with a high call volume to 311, but there are neighborhoods in the city where, for whatever reason, people may not report things to 311. If we relied on 311 call data alone, we could miss hot spots that needed attention.

To help eliminate blind spots, you need to draw in other inputs, pulling in other sources to validate your findings. In this case, we reached out to the mayor's Community Affairs Unit and other city officials who were intimately aware of the city and its neighborhoods and who were helping people across the city who had been affected by the storms. They reviewed our findings and offered refinement that highlighted areas not represented in the data. This ensured that we accounted for blind spots that may have resulted from relying on data alone.

UNDERSTAND HOW PROCESS AND DATA INTERACT

It's also important to understand how process and data interact. A good analyst cannot understand one without the other because in an operation, process creates data.

In the case of the flood mitigation, when a citizen called to report flooding, they picked up the phone, dialed 311, and spoke with a call taker. The call taker then asked questions to understand why the citizen was calling and what precisely they were trying to report to the city. Understanding how call takers identified what the caller was reporting allowed us to pull all of the data related to flooding. There were different types of calls that would offer us insight into locations of potential flooding. For example, a citizen might call to report a sewer backup in a basement, or a caller might report a street flooding condition. Each of these calls required different responses from the city. Sewer backups might require installation of backflow preventers and community outreach in the areas hardest hit. In contrast, to mitigate street flooding, the city might need to make improvements to catch basins or do an examination of the wastewater infrastructure of the area. It was critical as we looked at mountains of data to know the process to better understand how reports were classified in order to determine where in the city different types of flooding was occurring. Understanding these intricacies also allowed us to examine ways in which the city might have already responded so we were informed of what was already being done.

Let's take another process that might be familiar to more people—911. When citizens call 911 in an emergency, they initiate a process that deploys resources to help, whether police, fire, or EMS. At each step in the process, data are created when actions are taken and recorded in systems. Understanding the process that creates those data makes deeper analysis possible and provides an understanding of what the data actually means and what they can tell us.

For example, my team helped create a number of response-time reports at the FDNY. The agency had historically measured response time as the period from when the agency received notification of an emergency until the first responding unit arrived on the scene. The department used this important measure to manage its responses. However, there was also the processing time at the 911 call center from when an emergency call taker received the call to when it was transferred to the fire department. If you are the citizen needing help, that extra time, whether thirty seconds or one minute more, can seem like a lifetime. It's therefore critical to understand in detail how calls were routed from the moment someone in distress dialed 911to when a unit was on the scene in order to measure and tie all the data elements together.

To measure this full end-to-end response time, my team created and used process flow diagrams to understand every step that occurred from the time a citizen picked up the phone to dial 911 until the first emergency response unit had arrived on the scene. The diagrams gave us an understanding of the nuances of the data. For example, measuring the start of a call to 911 occurred when a call hit the system's switch and registered data with the telephone company's data systems. The diagrams allowed us to identify where in each process the various data systems captured timestamp data or other information. In this way, we could add each increment of time in the entire process of an emergency call.

Knowing what data is collected and reported helps an organization fully understand how to leverage insight on a process. Knowing all the data elements that are collected and how they are reported improves awareness and builds an organization's capacity for understanding.

MAKE THE DATA SING

Once your understanding is grounded in the process of a particular dataset, you need to make the data sing, organizing the data in a way that tells a story. Using tools to help visualize the data is vital to making data come alive, and it provides insights into what we see in the data. This can help decision makers find, focus on, and fix problems in a way that makes a difference in people's lives.

In the flooding example, thousands of dots (representing

311 calls) stacked on top of one another were not compelling and did not help us see any shape or form. So we reached out to the city's Department of Information Technology and Telecommunications, which had a geographic information systems (GIS) department, to see whether they could help us improve the plotting of the data for the thousands of calls to 311. Our thought was to map it in a way that would allow us to identify neighborhoods with the highest concentration of calls. They turned the dots into a density raster (aka heat map) with color variations that became darker where the data were more highly concentrated. The technique immediately helped us recognize the areas of the city that were experiencing the highest volume of calls. Visualizing the data this way caused the hot spots to jump off the page. We then knew where we had to focus—ten areas of the city that needed serious policy intervention to protect homes and property.

Using the correct tools to produce a picture that was compelling and that clarified what the data could tell us brought immediate attention to the problem areas. Our knowledge of various data tools allowed us to see the problem more clearly and to do what good analysis does: empowered us to take action!

INCREASE YOUR DATA CAPACITY

Because data is so important to having a meaningful

impact, help your organization increase its data capacity over time. Laying a solid foundation and establishing the basics, such as reports and notifications, takes a lot of time.

When building the NYC Department of Veterans' Services (discussed in chapter 8), for instance, we had no database of our own and only limited data on our target population, but we started digging for data and pulling it in. It took time, but we were able to start building reports and understanding veterans in NYC a little better—who they were, what they were like, and where they lived. The next level was to think about the needs of the various segments of the veteran population. This included what resources they needed or desired, and how the city could best serve them. Data capacity in government accumulates layer upon layer, one step at a time.

MAKING AN IMPACT

Having identified our focus areas, we reconvened our task force. Each agency came with a list of tools and resources that were potentially available to reduce flooding. The DEP discussed how stormwater mitigation starts at the street level with catch basins. Those become covered with debris during heavy rainfalls, and street flooding results. The DEP had programs to enlist an army of volunteers across the five boroughs who would keep catch basins clear during rainstorms to get the water to the pipelines.

Areas of the city that were more prone to street flooding could have additional catch basins installed of a different type that would also address the debris problem. In some areas, the DOT suggested that it might even be able to lower the street pavement a few inches to reveal more curb. Especially in areas where homes were below street level, this would mitigate the floodwaters flowing into homes. The DOB recommended that the city conduct outreach to building owners to educate the public on sewer backflow prevention devices that they could install to prevent water from flowing back into their homes. There was also discussion of diverting rainwater away from areas where it could damage property to areas that could be flooded during rain events, such as green fields and parks.

The team also brought several larger scale items to the table. The city was preparing to install tidal basin storm gates that essentially acted as backflow preventers to the entire system and was working to move up the timeline for completing that project. Several areas of the city that needed upgrades to stormwater infrastructure were prioritized for installation, although that was a long-term solution.

From there, joint teams from multiple agencies visited each hot spot, taking photos of areas hardest hit during a recent rainstorm, meeting with community leaders and property owners, and driving the streets to survey the infrastructure of roads and catch basins in each area. Their dozens of photographs provided a better sense of the situation on the ground to the task force, which then dissected the situation in each neighborhood. With photos, survey information, and on-the-ground truth from our team members, the task force developed a strong understanding of what was happening in each area. As a result, we were able to propose the actions that were most suitable in each hot spot, and the experts from each of the city agencies could propose how their agency might alleviate the flooding. We packaged this work together as the basis of our recommendations to the mayor's office.

KEY TAKEAWAYS

Data can help municipalities make smarter decisions—that is, identify how to invest scarce resources where they will have the greatest impact on the most people (more bang for the buck). To make the best decisions, first build maturity in the most basic levels of data intelligence and then add layers as data capacity is shaped.

In the case of flood mitigation, we asked questions until we got a clearer picture of what and where the problem was. We then leveraged data tools to bring a different perspective to the project and help us clarify our objectives. We ensured our data analysis was done with consideration of the process behind the data to understand precisely what the data represented. We also consulted community experts to ensure that data matched the on-the-ground truth and that we weren't unintentionally leaving out those not represented in the data, thereby avoiding the data blind spots. Pulling in experts from city agencies then allowed us to decide what actions to take. From there, rather than creating a campaign across the entire city, we honed in, using all the data we had collected, to identify areas that were experiencing a disproportionate amount of damage. We drove programming and response more deeply there than if we had tried to do the same across the entire city.

After understanding where you are and where you want to go, the next step of your process roadmap is to plan your route from your starting point to your end point.

CHAPTER 3

PLAN THE ROUTE

When you have a project, program, or initiative and need to determine the most important elements for moving it forward, make a plan. This chapter helps you prioritize, organize, and create a plan that will get stuff done.

"Plans are worthless, but planning is everything."

—DWIGHT D. EISENHOWER

The sunlight glinted off the Hudson River late in the day in early spring. I was sitting at my desk when my boss called and asked me to stop by her office at the other end of the hallway of our twenty-second-floor perch in lower Manhattan. I walked to her office and took a seat opposite her. She looked up from some notes.

"I want you to go out to our enforcement unit and see how we can improve reporting," she said.

I was a deputy commissioner with the NYC TLC, the agency that regulates taxis and for-hire vehicular transportation in NYC. It was the early part of 2016, a time when the industries that the TLC regulated were experiencing explosive growth with the advent of app-based services such as Uber and Lyft. In NYC, there were 13,500 yellow taxis as well as 42,000 livery, black car, and limousine services (those from companies such as Uber, Lyft, and other community car services). Borough taxis (also known as green taxis) were making their debut, serving the outer boroughs beyond the city's main business core. In all, these industries provided nearly a million trips each day to New Yorkers and visitors and were the third largest mover of people in NYC behind subways and buses.

The TLC was on the heels of what had been a very contentious summer as the city determined how to better regulate app-based companies such as Uber and Lyft. These industry disrupters were upending regulatory frameworks in municipalities across the globe as cities struggled to keep pace with a relentless barrage of change. The summer of 2015 had turned particularly combative when NYC started receiving data from these app companies (as reporting regulations required that trip records be sent to the TLC). When I joined the team, the TLC had recently passed a rules package requiring for-hire vehicle companies to submit their trip records electronically. The purpose was to help with TLC enforcement activity (to ensure that only licensed drivers and vehicles were on the road) and to inform policy making of trip demand and supply of for-hire transportation services across the city. It would also give the TLC insight into how many vehicles and what type (wheelchair-accessible vehicles, for example) were actively providing service (NYC Taxi and Limousine Commission 2014). For the first time, a municipal government would know when, where, and how many trips occurred in various parts of the city.

These new data records provided insight into exactly what the city faced in terms of the number of trips these licensed vehicles took on a daily basis. And even though the city and municipalities across the globe struggled to determine the best regulatory framework moving forward, a freeze on the growth of the app companies was deemed necessary to allow the issue to be studied. So controversial was this idea that Uber even created a de Blasio option in its app (named after NYC's mayor) that showed imaginary wait times of twenty-five minutes (exaggerating the impact on wait times of proposed regulation that did not allow these companies to do exactly what they wanted how they wanted) (Tepper 2015).

During all this, a federal judge ruled that the TLC could no longer seize vehicles from drivers suspected of illegal street hail or livery services in places such as airports and tourist hot spots. That decision hampered a significant tool in the TLC enforcement arsenal. The TLC Enforcement Unit (EU) fulfilled the agency's role of ensuring that the various actors in these industries all played by the same rules and that nonlicensed actors were kept out. There had always been many bad actors who illegally picked up and transported passengers, and this affected the overall health of each of the service sectors. The EU, an approximately 150-person quasi-police force under the auspices of the TLC's Uniformed Services Bureau (USB), worked to ensure that licensed drivers and vehicles providing ride services all followed the city's rules and regulations. The federal ruling had crippled one of the TLC's most effective enforcement tools, and the commissioner was interested in learning how data could be leveraged to help improve enforcement actions.

THE CENTER OF OPERATIONS: THE SITUATION ROOM

To meet my boss's request, I convened a task force of several individuals from the agency who were able to dedicate time each week to the work we were about to do. I and another individual would principally oversee the project, working full time on the task force for the next sixty days. Others would dedicate time a couple of days weekly. Representatives from tech, legal, policy, and administration would analyze the EU's activities to better understand how they aligned with the TLC's strategy.

The EU was housed in Woodside, Queens, in a part of the city remote from the TLC's headquarters. When I reported to Woodside for the first time, the unit's leadership had already reserved a large classroom for me and the task force. The nearly empty classroom was perfect! The walls were blank—just what we needed.

In any major project, it's helpful to have a situation room, war room, or operations center. You need a place where you can lay out all the information you collect and see what story emerges. It doesn't have to be an entire room. It's just a place where you can let information marinate, whether it's a desk, a conference room, or simply a digital note—any place where you can step back and look at the problem, observing all the elements of a situation and see where the pieces do not quite make sense or fit together.

From our situation room, we started by defining the project's purpose, but the goal line was somewhat nebulous. Somehow, we had to define what information the EU already collected and what information the EU could collect. We then had to determine how to improve what information was reported to the boss and how. As the leader of the task force, my job was to determine the nature of point B and plan a route to it. After arranging tables and chairs, finding a printer, and setting up our laptops, the task force got to work.

In my experience, the path from the start point to the end point takes shape as you *collect, organize,* and *assess* information about the operations of the unit, as discussed in chapter 1. Then, after looking at leading practices and organizations that overcame similar challenges, you can chart a path—in this case, determine the ideal that the TLC should strive for and learn exactly how to leverage data in practical, everyday terms.

TALK TO THE EXPERTS

To chart the most effective path forward, it's critical that you talk to the experts—the people within the relevant organization—in the data collection phase.

People from within the organization can provide a fresh perspective on your particular project or issue to help you understand where you might make changes. Relying on those who are familiar with the overall organization but are somewhat removed from your problem can help you identify potential improvements and focus on key areas. This can also be a much lower-cost option than hiring consultants, although it is not appropriate in all situations. When you can leverage in-house resources, no contracts are required, and members of the team already have an understanding of the overall organization, saving time and money.

In our case, our task force talked to as many EU staff as

possible, both uniformed officers and administrative and support staff, anyone who played a role in the workings, processes, or procedures of the EU and might have a tidbit of information that could help us understand the unit's work.

We held dozens of discussions to begin painting a picture of the unit and its operation. We pulled in the enforcement squads (teams of approximately twelve people each) and conducted group interviews. My assistant and I scheduled these meetings for sixty to ninety minutes and invited the squads to our classroom. We asked that only the squads and squad leaders attend, eliminating anyone else in the leadership chain. We wanted to provide a forum in which interviewees felt free to express their views without fear of reprisal. For this same reason, it's also important to protect interviewees' anonymity. I always tell those who provide insights that we will never share their attributed, verbatim responses with decision makers.

It is important to note that operational assessments and interviews with key stakeholders, particularly in a group interview setting, can quickly turn into a gripe session. You want to create a forum in which people feel free to express their viewpoints, in which they may veer off topic but lead you to important insights that you might not have discovered otherwise. However, you also want to keep the conversation moving in a direction that provides information on your main topic area. Guiding this type of meeting to fully obtain the desired information takes practice, and only an active meeting facilitator gets it right.

You should start each meeting by introducing yourself and explain why you are there and what you are trying to learn. In our case, we indicated that we were very interested in how the team captured data in the field with handhelds, how they conducted certain processes and procedures, where they thought the TLC should change, and whether any tools could improve field operations.

Without hesitation, each squad provided us with extensive information on the greatest challenges facing the teams, as well as their perspectives on where the EU was operating well overall and where improvements could be made. All these suggestions and insights were recorded.

We continued our assessment, toured the facilities, and scheduled ride-alongs. Each bit of information we collected contributed to a process map of how the unit worked, how and what data it collected along the way, and where those data elements were stored (whether on paper or electronically). (See graphic 3.1 for this process flow map.)

Figure 3.1: Sample Process Flow Reporting

SVR Member 5.05 — Divides squad reports across the unit's personnel

SVR Member 5.06 — Verifies that the information in the reports match what is contained in the car stop sheets

SVR Member 5.07 — If incomplete, sends MIS an email saying back-office information is incomplete

MIS 5.08 — Researches and corrects the information when possible

SVR Member 5.08 — Verifies all information in ESAP is complete and matches Daily Squad Report and approves them

SVR Unit 5.09 — Creates recurring and ad hoc reports as requested

SVR Unit 5.10 — Various reports

B Page 14

SVR Member 5.01 — Pulls roll call packet from the lockbox in the captain's office

SVR Member 5.02 — Checks each squad packet to ensure it is complete

SVR Member 5.03 — Logs confiscated materials information into Credentials Database (Access)

SVR Member 5.04 — Generates a transmittal file to send to S&E for equipment violations and to Licensing for license credentials

A

TLC-generated summons? — NO → **C Page 14**

YES → **TLC-generated field summons or administrative summons?** — FIELD → (to 5.01) / ADMINISTRATIVE → **D Page 14**

Start

SVR Reports

| Roll Call Database 3.11 | Roll Call Database 5.11 | Roll Call Database 5.12 | Roll Call Database 5.13 | Access-SVR 5.14 | Roll Call Database/SVR/Ajud 5.15 | Roll Call Database/SVR/Ajud 5.16 | Access-SVR Squad Activity 5.17 |
| Daily Squad Report | | Precincts Report | Weekly Productivity Report | VACC STATS Breakdowns by Summs by Prec | Deputy Commissioner Weekly Productivity Report | Deputy Commissioner Weekly Memo | Monthly Metrics |

| Access-SVR Squad Activity 5.18 | Access-SVR Squad Activity 5.19 | Various |
| CPR | Hotel Weekly Report | Ad Hoc Reports |

We also evaluated the reports they completed and submitted them to TLC headquarters to determine whether the collected and reported data elements contained any redundancies.

Beyond the squads, we solicited input from other experts throughout the organization, including representatives from operations, administration, policy, legal, and other areas. They all lent their perspectives on the problem at hand, and we ended up shaping recommendations based on their experiences and understanding of the issues. We interviewed all the office personnel and the reporting team, sitting with them to see how they organized and managed data and how they created reports for the higher-ups.

We spoke with squad leaders and the chiefs who oversaw multiple squads to determine how they conducted business. We met with the technology team to understand how the databases were maintained and organized, and we wanted to get their perspective on the biggest challenges and opportunities related to the enforcement team. They understood the complexities of using handhelds and rolling out technology updates or upgrades, as well as how to consolidate data in a repository or data warehouse. Their input was critical in helping us analyze and provide recommendations that were grounded and feasible. We met with radio room staff to see the process by which EU officers requisitioned radio equipment, and we met with the technology staff who outfitted the building with computer terminals.

All along the way, we took in-depth notes, snapped pictures, and recorded anything we learned or needed to better understand. These activities allowed us to identify some of the key challenges facing EU personnel and how they impacted the team's ability to collect data.

Having experts from various areas of the agency proved to be invaluable. It ensured that our recommendations acknowledged the agency's realities in each area and were well thought out and quite feasible (in terms of cost, level of effort to implement, length of time to implement, etc.). Furthermore, our interviews of employees and key staff had revealed their thoughts on how to improve operations. Simply by engaging and asking the right questions, we were finding solutions and potential ways to implement them from the team.

ORGANIZE YOUR INFORMATION AND LOOK FOR PATTERNS

After collecting information from the experts, you can begin to organize and assess. At this stage, look for patterns. The items that multiple people report across teams or within an organization usually indicate the pain points that need attention.

We consolidated our written notes and ordered the various insights, comments, and ideas into an extensive list. We organized them by topic and began to see (mainly by the number of comments made or the intensity with which they were made) the topic areas that represented the biggest pain points. This information would help us prioritize the topic areas that demanded the greatest level of research on how to move forward.

We also collected and organized notes on any items that were raised but were not germane to our project. These out-of-scope notes provided valuable information to leadership. Although the issues and ideas may have been outside the scope of our project, the unit leadership might nevertheless have been interested in delving into them.

After collecting information from interviews, process flows, and reports, we conducted our ride-alongs, which allowed us to investigate the patterns and compare points of confusion on paper with what we saw on the ground. Having gathered as much information as possible about the process ahead of time, we knew precisely what to look for and what questions to ask. This made our ride-along time more valuable because the learning was much more specific. It clarified our understanding where it had been hazy in the collection stage. The ride-alongs would not have been as fruitful had they been our first introduction to TLC enforcement actions. We also gained an appreciation of how risky the job was for enforcement personnel. Making regular traffic stops of TLC-licensed vehicles or those illegally providing for-hire transportation was a very dangerous business.

As we collected new information throughout the process, we used the walls of our classroom to hang our notes, sample documents, process flows, and so on, which allowed us to view what we were seeing from different angles. Quite literally, we could step back and examine what we saw to find where pain points or redundancies existed, where things could be streamlined, or where they simply made no sense. For example, we posted along one of the walls all the reports that officers were required to create during a shift, which allowed us to see the massive volume of information, the various forms needed, and the areas of duplication where the same information was reported multiple times.

LEARN FROM OTHERS: LEADING PRACTICES/ LITERATURE REVIEW

After establishing your starting point, a leading practices/literature review is the crucial element in creating a path from that start point to your desired end point. Once you have identified pain points and areas clearly needing change, you can leverage models from other organizations, jurisdictions, or teams that have succeeded in doing something similar. Learning from them and how they approached a problem creates a link between where you are and where you should go.

Interviewing those who have successfully tackled similar projects allows you to apply what worked for them while learning about the challenges they faced. In dozens of leading practices interviews, I have found that almost everyone will openly share what they have faced in terms of wins and lessons learned. They readily share how they would do things differently the next time, things they wish they had known, and what to do or avoid.

These interviews also inspire strategic thinking. Talking to others who have done interesting and complex things usually stimulates creativity among your own project team and in your own thinking. Look for these conversations and recognize the value that they provide to you and your project. At the end of the day, every boss I have ever worked for has asked some form of this question: "What are other people doing?"

Obviously, there is no one-size-fits-all solution to operational challenges, but there are also few new ideas. Copy what works for others, looking for patterns to identify those practices worth replicating. Take the ideas and models of others, apply them to your issue, and let that drive your recommendations. The military, for example, promotes a culture that openly shares tools, techniques, and procedures. Don't be afraid to find tools that work for others, refine them, make them your own, and put them to work on your project or problem set.

Whenever conducting a leading practices review, it is helpful to organize your findings in a leading practices matrix to display the main findings from your research in a succinct way. I generally create a table with a different leading practice heading each column, and several rows including information such as a description of the practice, its benefits and challenges, and the extent to which your current organization performs the leading practice. For an example of a leading practices matrix, see graphic 3.2.

Figure 3.2: Sample Leading Practices Matrix

Practice	Data and Descriptor Standardization	Historical Data Protection	Data Consolidation	Process Automation
Description	• Standards should be enforced as early as possible. • Data should be correct, clean, complete, formatted, and verified.	• Past data should be input and saved within system. • When deciding which data to keep, data volume versus data value must be considered.	• Consolidate as much data as possible into a single source. • Allows all users to see content based on their roles and permissions. • Make data readily available (e.g., through intranet).	• Automate as many processes as possible.
Benefits	• Creates highly granular database. • Granularity is necessary to create specific terms. • Specific terms enable accurate data analysis. • If started early, this process significantly reduces manual effort later on.	• Ensures that meaningful analysis can continue without interruption. • Prevents loss of information.	• Can be time-saving: users enter data only once as opposed to multiple times. • Allows for information sharing. • Simplifies management of complex data. • Facilitates exploration and analysis.	• Minimizes manual errors and inefficiency. • Reduces labor-intensive and repetitive activities. • Data becomes streamlined.
Challenges	• Implementation can be challenging. • Parameters must be set to ensure data is entered in the proper format. • Perpetually ongoing process.	• Can be time-consuming. • If historical data is kept and never used, can take up valuable space and decelerate system.	• Data from one system may not align well with another because of a missing value(s). • Outside expertise may be necessary, which is costly.	• Integration with current system may be difficult and expensive. • Some degree of human control is lost.
My Organization Leverages	○	◑	●	◑

Key

○ Does Not Leverage   ◑ Somewhat Leverages   ● Fully Leverages

LEADING PRACTICES/LITERATURE REVIEW IN ACTION

After establishing where we were through collect/organize/ assess, we turned our attention to how we could leverage data to improve our understanding of enforcement. For this, we conducted a review of leading practices, scouring the world for other organizations that had faced similar challenges to see what we could learn from them.

First, I surveyed the task force to learn what projects and programs they were familiar with, either in NYC government or elsewhere, that might provide good insight into improving data decision-making and enforcement operations. The team offered a couple of suggestions that became our first stops in reviewing leading practices. I also did extensive online research to find projects and programs that had been recognized in the news, by academic institutions, or had won awards indicating that they might offer a worthy model. This gave us the following list of projects worth researching.

NYPD (NEW YORK POLICE DEPARTMENT) DOMAIN AWARENESS SYSTEM (DAS)

This platform provided a comprehensive view of potential criminal activity and developing threats to security, giving officials a way to aggregate and analyze data from surveillance cameras, 911 calls, license plate readers, radiation detectors, previous crime reports, and multiple public safety databases. Operators could use the system's interactive dashboard to quickly pull and correlate public safety, geospatial, chronological, and other information that might be relevant to a specific alert. At the time, a mobile version had recently been developed and rolled out.

NYPD HUNCHLAB

This predictive policing technology forecasted crime based on temporal patterns, such as time of day, time of week, day of month, seasonality, weather, environmental risk factors (the location of bars, bus stops, etc.), socioeconomic indicators, and historic crime levels. In the summer of 2015, HunchLab was being tested by three police precincts for a two-year period. It helped police departments understand and respond more effectively to crime using the resources already available to them.

NYC COMPTROLLER'S BUREAU OF LAW AND ADJUSTMENT CLAIMSTAT

This program identified trends in claims made against the city, enabling analysts to highlight troubling developments and best practices. The program identified claims that led to costly settlements and judgments across the city before they become multimillion-dollar cases. The NYC comptroller used the program's findings to coordinate interagency committees that worked together to identify potential solutions.

PHILADELPHIA POLICE DEPARTMENT SMART POLICING PROGRAM

This federally funded program put officers through a rigorous two-week crime science program at Temple University. It used police officers who were familiar with departmental culture and trained them in the use of Excel, crime mapping systems, and methods for strategically collecting and utilizing information from surveys.

NYC MAYOR'S OFFICE OF DATA ANALYTICS (MODA), DATABRIDGE

This program automated data feeds from over fifty source systems in twenty agencies and external organizations. The data were warehoused and merged, permitting the city to perform cross-agency analysis and enabling NYC analysts to examine data from across city agencies to effectively address crime, public safety, and quality-of-life issues.

To start the process, my trusty analyst worked the internet to find contacts for these projects or programs and to schedule conversations with them so we could ask questions and learn. It was sometimes a scavenger hunt, reaching out to people and asking whether they could put us in contact with the person who managed or oversaw the project. If anyone on our team knew someone connected to the project, they were able to make a warm introduction to get us in the door for a conversation. Otherwise, we had to make phone calls, reach out by email to contacts we found online, and do investigative work until we found the right person.

We also scoured the internet for information about these specific projects and programs. This provided helpful insights into what the project or program was about, what problem it was trying to solve, and its challenges, but mostly it told us about its successes and what it accomplished. By diving in prior to our interviews, we were able to take the conversation deeper and discuss the nuts-and-bolts items with the person who oversaw the project and lived in the trenches, day in and day out, to get it done.

SAMPLE LEADING PRACTICES QUESTIONS

Describe the system you have now and how it works.

What alternatives, if any, did you consider, and why did you choose your current system?

What can your agency do now that it couldn't do before? [Assessing strength]

What do you wish the system could do that it currently cannot do or does not do well enough? [Assessing weakness]

What changes have you seen from implementing the new system? This could be employee satisfaction, hiring trends, results on the ground, and so forth.

Positive changes?

Negative changes?

Anything that you didn't expect?

Under different conditions, would you have done things differently?

What do you foresee in the future?

In terms of results?

In terms of systems: Acquiring more? Maintaining the current one?

What is the broader significance of this new system for your organization/city?

We also had questions specific to each program that we intended to interview for our leading practices.

For the NYPD, we asked:

- Do the systems (or the information they contain) cohere or do they operate independently?
- What smartphones have you given to your officers?
- If cops have a single smartphone, do they see both CompStat and DAS?

For the Philadelphia PD, we asked:

- What does the course look like?
- Is it taught after hours or during work time?
- What can you tell me about the duration of the course?
- Do the officers have any equipment on the ground to access this information or do they do it at the office?
- Do the officers like the course?
- What feedback have you received?
- Have there been any changes in employment and/or turnover since you introduced this program?

For the Mayor's Office of Data Analytics, we asked whether there had been any unintended positive or negative consequences of their program.

When conducting these interviews, we kept the following things in mind: Let the interviewee do 80 percent of the talking. Avoid yes/no and why questions. Press them to explain what was going on: "What was happening at the time?" Learn about the system that they built and were using, not the concept or design they were trying to build. Keep probing. Don't accept the first response.

In each of these interviews as well as the literature review we conducted, we parsed out the methods or practices that we wanted to consider replicating in our own design for a pathway forward for the EU. We would prioritize these items for inclusion in our own implementation plan for operational data management, and we highlighted the benefits and challenges of each practice. We also discussed with our leading practice contacts the challenges we were finding in our project to find out how they might have tackled similar issues.

PRESENT YOUR FINDINGS

Once we completed our interviews, process flows, ride-alongs, surveys, and leading practices review, the task force convened to organize the information into a comprehensive list of recommendations on how the EU could move forward. This was our route to the desired end state. Because of our in-depth analysis of the unit's current status, most of us had now become subject matter experts on its operations, in some ways more than the unit's members because we could step back and view it holistically.

When you present your findings, it's important to organize your recommendations in a way that allows your report to stand alone. Include enough data and information to allow a reader to quickly digest the main takeaways and understand how you arrived at your recommendations. Share the documentation. Put in sample documents and pictures and fewer words. In my projects, I found that creating process flows and documenting interviews, ride-alongs, and surveys helped me to break an operation into bite-size pieces. I have also found that those products are very valuable in themselves.

Documenting a business or operational process at a fine level of detail has many uses and, at the very least, helps managers recognize how work is actually being done, which often differs from how they thought it was done. In this project, we documented everything we learned and provided the findings to our leadership, giving them a reference that allowed them to quickly digest how things operated in a large, complex operation. Documentation also provides a reference for future use. Obviously, operations change over time and documentation grows stale, but organizing and recording all the collected information helps leaders who may need to reference it in the future.

Also, in documenting the findings and recommendations in a final report, we followed a format that I have found works in both government and the military. The headings may differ slightly, but the purpose of the formatting is similar. We started with a purpose slide to restate the problem that the project was addressing and remind the audience/client of what this was all about. Seems simple, but it is important to restate what the project is (and is not) and to focus the recommendations that follow.

SAMPLE OUTLINE

Purpose or Problem Statement

Background

Summary of Findings

Summary of Work

Details of Findings

Leading Practices

Models

Recommendations

Roadmap

Annexes

Notes/Documentation of Interviews

Notes/Documentation of Ride-Alongs

Notes/Documentation of Surveys

Process Flows or Other Assessments

From our list of many findings, we assessed how we could improve the situation, and we included potential options for addressing each finding. In this assessment, we indicated how a solution might be implemented, the required level of effort, the likely cost, and its potential impact. Recruiting the agency's subject matter experts from technology, policy, legal, and other areas paid dividends as they were able to delve into estimating these details. We also asked our leading practices interviewees about methods of implementation, how they kept costs low, how they contracted with vendors, and other implementation details. This process produced a detailed list of recommendations, from those that were low cost and easily implemented to those that were high cost and hard to implement.

Generally, it is helpful to provide a roadmap—a plan for how and when each of the recommendations should be implemented, such as a timeline showing durations, dependencies (when one task relies on another for completion before it can commence), and start and end dates. A roadmap is critical in providing leadership with an approach for implementing the recommendations and step-by-step directions for the order in which implementation should occur. In other words, the roadmap provides the how for getting to the end point. Some recommendations can be quickly implemented and at low or no cost, also known as quick wins. Quick wins should be implemented immediately. Other recommendations may have multiple phases, with the foundational elements of each recommendation needing to be implemented before the subsequent phases can be. Do this first, then do this, then this. The roadmap gives leadership your framework for getting it all done and knowing what to do first, next, and so on.

MAKING AN IMPACT

Our final deliverables included twenty pages of detailed process flows that had never before been documented to such an extent. These included seven high-level operational processes and an additional five subprocesses with detailed action steps that an employee took in each process. We also created a database and reports inventory—that is, a comprehensive list of all the data systems, data elements, and reports that the unit relied on throughout its process. We tied each of these systems and reports to our operational process flows for easy reference to where they occurred in the EU's day-to-day work. In the reports review, we listed and defined all the reports that the unit created, the frequency of each report, its purpose, and its source. Our final documentation included a sample of each report, where the report was filed, how it was formatted, and so on, ensuring that future readers of our work would not have to look for examples of the things we had identified.

From this work, we created a list of the top recommendations we identified for improving operations. This product described how the unit could best move to point B. For example, among our findings was that the team's handhelds presented significant challenges to its ability to complete the work efficiently. We then broke this down into specific findings related to areas where the handheld technology could be improved. We also provided detailed information and screenshots or photographs of the issue so that anyone reading our report could clearly see the problem. The recommendation for how to improve (point B) was inspired by our interviews. Most of the employees provided significant insight on how each of these areas could improve. Additionally, through our leading practices review, we determined how others were doing similar work.

KEY TAKEAWAYS

This exercise and many operational assessments like it gave me some key takeaways that will help you conduct meaningful analysis and provide a robust, realistic, and feasible roadmap for your boss or other stakeholder.

First, listen to your own people. Engaging with stakeholders (through interviews, surveys, focus groups, etc.) provides much of the inspiration for improvement in an operation, project, or program. You'll discover a great deal about people and how to make things better by soliciting their viewpoints and asking how they would do things differently if they could. That's where the magic happens! Be sure to look for patterns among their insights.

Then, always conduct leading practices research. Thoroughly review the literature, studies, and leading practices to find solutions to each of those pain points and models worthy of exploration and replication. The leading practices research, if done thoroughly, will allow you to take the ideas of others and put them to work for yourself.

With a planned route in place, your next step is to stay on the path.

CHAPTER 4

STAY ON THE PATH

Once your project is underway, some simple tools, techniques, and procedures will help you get things done and anticipate issues and challenges before they arise.

"To plan is human, to implement divine."

—UNKNOWN

I had been out of the office from the FDNY for my annual two-week military training. When I returned, I was pulled into my boss's office and told I would be overseeing one of the department's most visible technology projects, with a $30 million capital budget. While I was away, there had been a meeting between city hall and members of the FDNY, and city hall had instructed the department to complete this project as quickly as possible. Mayor Bloomberg had pledged that it would be finished before his term was up, and the deputy mayor who oversaw the FDNY was relentless in his pursuit of closing this project. I was now on the agency side of managing projects. I was now the director of grant monitoring for the FDNY. After three years as an analyst with the Mayor's Office of Operations, it was time to enter city agency life.

The project, known as the Risk-Based Inspection System, provided an application that tracked building inspections by the Bureau of Fire Operations across NYC. At the time, fire companies performed nine hours of building inspections each week (three hours, three days a week). These inspections ensured that the companies were familiar with the buildings in their administrative districts.[2] The companies looked for life safety hazards (e.g., rubbish piled in the basement, locks and chains on doors, nonworking exit signs and fire escapes, etc.) and other special information about the building. They also visited buildings that required recurring inspections, such as schools and hospitals, as well as buildings under construction or demolition. Further technical inspections were handled by a different division within the FDNY, the Bureau of Fire Prevention. Once building inspections were completed, fire officers updated and tracked the information on building cards that were kept in the office. (See graphic 4.1 for an example of a building card.)

---

2   Each fire company had an area that it covered for administrative purposes, such as building inspections.

Figure 4.1: Sample Building Card

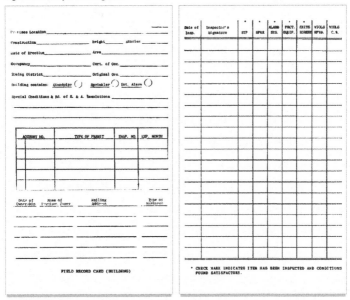

FIELD RECORD CARD (BUILDING)

* CHECK MARK INDICATES ITEM HAS BEEN INSPECTED AND CONDITIONS FOUND SATISFACTORY.

This project also included a risk model that was conceived as a result of the Deutsche Bank Building fire. As part of the city's investigation and recommendations following that tragic fire, it was determined that the FDNY needed to conduct building inspections based on risk, not merely the cyclical process they had followed to this point. There was an early version of the risk model, built by a consultant, in the application although it needed updating as new data were increasingly available. As a result of the Deutsche Bank Building fire, there had been a major push to supply the FDNY with building data from other city agencies. The department had more and more information about each building in the city, which would allow data scientists to create a more compelling model to determine which buildings were more likely to have a fire or life safety incident. Given this, the department needed to identify a way to redesign the current risk model.

There was already a project plan and a capable team overseeing the project. What was needed was someone dedicated to bridging the gap between the agency's leadership and city hall on a day-to-day basis, keeping everyone on the same page and the project on path. Although I was not an IT expert, I had spent three years in the Mayor's Office of Operations and, at that point, had been at the FDNY for over a year. I was as good a choice as any to support this project and navigate the intricacies of city hall.

TAKE STOCK

Anytime you come on board an in-progress project—as well as periodically through the lifetime of a project—take the time to pause and evaluate where you are. Take stock of what's going well and what still needs to be done.

The project as I found it was progressing well but lacked some key components that city hall was particularly interested in. There was no internal team in the department to enhance the risk model, so we would have to look for external support for that element of the project until we built the agency's Analytics Unit, which would then be able to do the research. The project also needed a training and rollout timeline to train fire officers in how the new application worked and how it would affect their building inspection operations, as well as to provide help desk support for implementing the overall program.

We also needed a clear definition of project success. My understanding was that the project would develop and deploy an application for use by the agencies over 2,300 fire officers across more than 200 administrative districts. The first version would have baseline functionality, but additional enhancements would be considered and implemented in future builds. The project team had distilled the list of project requirements to thirteen must-haves, and they anticipated it taking eleven months to complete the build. To identify those requirements, a battalion fire chief had been asked to pilot the program. His battalion officers used the application and provided weekly feedback to the project team throughout the project's life. This proved invaluable, and with the chief's feedback and leadership, the project team was able to identify the "must haves," "nice to haves," and "can waits" in terms of the application's development and rollout. We would focus first on the must-haves, and once they were built and tested, the training team would roll out the application in a phased approach to all fire officers across the city while the technical team continued to make enhancements to the project. From these conversations and meetings, I now knew our start point. It was time to connect the dots.

CREATE A DETAILED PROJECT PLAN

Creating a detailed project plan is always necessary. It's a pain, but it ensures that you stay on track with the project matching the timeline as closely as possible.

In my first job in the Mayor's Office of Operations, one of the senior policy advisors I supported pushed me to include every single step in a project plan. As a result, throughout my career, I consistently created detailed project plans that considered the full amount of time required to complete a particular task. For example, drafting a report required the actual writing, sending it out for review, waiting for the reviewers to conduct the review, making changes based on the review, recirculating a second edit, making final changes, distributing the final draft to decision makers for sign-off, and submitting the draft for design work, publication, and so on. For these steps, thinking at the transactional level assigned a timeframe to each step, and even broad estimates contributed to an accurate overall timeline. This kind of detailed planning was not always fun, but it simplified project management and paid dividends as I moved forward.

A savvy project manager uses the project plan to keep everyone on task and on the same page. Ensure that every task has a project owner, a due date, and an executive sponsor or manager who will ensure it is adhered to.

For the Risk-Based Inspection System, every task had an owner at the management level, meaning that either I, the project manager, the technical lead, or the training lead was responsible and accountable for it. In my career, I have attended hundreds of meetings in which next steps were proposed but no one owned the next step. We avoided this pitfall by ensuring that every task had an owner as well as a due date. Our project plan indicated when each task was due and from whom. I included the parent task from the project plan on the dashboard that we used to track when the items were due. This is known as a Gantt chart. (See graphic 4.2 for a sample implementation timeline Gantt chart.)

Figure 4.2: Sample Implementation Timeline

Training Tasks	Sep 2012	Oct 2012	Nov 2012	Dec 2012	Jan 2013	Feb 2013
Instructor and Mentor	03–21					
Division 6		05–16	35% of units complete			
Division 7		19–30 ★				
Division 8 (and SOC)			03–14	> 50% of units complete		
Division 1			17–28 ★			
Division 3			31–11			
Division 11				14–25	> 75% of units complete	
Division 15				28–08 ★		
Division 13					11–22	100% of units complete
Division 14					25–08 ★✔	
Ongoing Monitoring and Support						

★ Milestone   ✔ Completed Task

Reviewing the individual tasks will not be fun, and doing so in a meeting can be excruciating, but it is effective. Find ways to pull this tool into your weekly dashboard, communicating the tasks that were completed in the previous time period and those upcoming with a due date in the next.

Planning at this level of detail generally ensures that a project remains on schedule. There will always be bumps in the road, but taking time on the front end to get the details right and develop a project plan with a precise level of detail provides a reasonable expectation of when the project will be completed.

USE PLANNING TOOLS: MICROSOFT PROJECT

Creating such detailed plans is nearly impossible without planning tools, so invest in and train yourself on how to use Microsoft Project or a similar tool. Knowing how to organize and communicate the tracking of a project in a powerful tool is an invaluable skill and worth the investment of taking a class to master it.

I found that the strongest aspect of such tools is that they enable you to see how each step of a project plan impacts the timeline and when the overall project will be complete. This is valuable when you need to understand what happens when the timeline for an individual task changes. I found that many tasks can be absorbed within a project plan. For example, if a project will take one year and one of the tasks will be delayed, impacting subsequent tasks, project management tools allow the project's dependencies to be identified in such a way that a project manager can determine which subtasks can continue on schedule. In this way, a project can be managed at the bite size, and what would otherwise seem like a major project timeline change can be managed in smaller transactional pieces.

For the Risk-Based Inspection System, I used Microsoft Project for project planning as almost everyone in the department would have access to the program. This would allow me to create a draft project plan and share it with the technical leadership and training chief to get their input and refinement. Having made similar project plans before, I knew how to drop in details quickly to get us started and focused. The technical team had a timeline for building each component of the thirteen technical requirements to full implementation, including testing, user acceptance, and all the other pieces of the technical build.

A training plan had not been established yet, but I knew that the training chief wanted to create a plan that would allow us to train one division at a time. I put on my military cap and started to consider how that would look and the potential timeline, not looking to get all the details absolutely correct but rather to start the planning. Giving the team a draft plan to react to would inspire the detailed planning that was needed to create a solid, overall project plan.

From there, I combined the technical and training plans into a large master project plan. Using planning tools, I calculated the overall timeline of the project, and we added a few weeks of contingencies for the unforeseen events and problems that inevitably arise.

DETERMINE GOVERNANCE OF THE PROJECT

The governance of a project matters. It may not be the most exciting topic, but it is vital to give some thought to and define how the project will be managed strategically and day to day. Establish at the front end of a project who has the authority to make what types of decisions, who will be notified when certain critical actions take place, and how changes will be made to a project's timeline, budget, or other resources.

It doesn't have to be overly complicated, but everyone needs to buy in. This will pay huge dividends when, in the bustle of a project or program, a crisis arises and needs a decision. You will know where to go and how to keep the project on track if you already have a process in place.

For this project, we created a simple project governance protocol that all the stakeholders agreed to, which was important for establishing who had the authority to approve changes to the project's timeline, budget, resources, and so forth. We built an organizational chart showing who was a member of the steering committee, who reported to whom, and who made decisions in regard to the project's budget and timeline. Under a certain dollar amount, the latter fell to the agency's executive manager, while above a certain threshold, it went to the steering committee, who made the decision and then informed the deputy mayor. We also determined the thresholds at which changes required approval and notification. For example, any change that impacted the timeline by less than two weeks would be approved at the agency level as it was considered negligible and did not require approvals or external communication to city hall. A change with a two-week impact or greater, however, required approval by the project's steering committee, which would review, discuss, determine how to move forward, and then recommend a course of action to city hall. We also defined who made decisions at the agency, who our point person was at city hall, and who was on the steering committee that made executive decisions.

Establishing this structure at the get-go took the guesswork out of it and provided clarity when issues arose. Thus, what might otherwise have been critical items became routine matters for which we had a means to manage their impacts.

ESTABLISH A BATTLE RHYTHM

Equally important to the plans and tools for tracking the project's success is establishing a battle rhythm for the project, defined as a cycle of meetings and timelines that are followed to keep an organization or team on task. For example, many military units follow a twenty-four-hour battle rhythm that shows when working groups, meetings, briefings, and reports are due. This gets the team into a rhythm of making updates and sending in daily reports, which becomes second nature to them.

Most of us have battle rhythms although we may not recognize them as such. Intentionally designing a battle rhythm ensures that all the stakeholders of a large project are aware of the project and its status.

Creating a battle rhythm also builds predictability and structure into fast-paced environments that can quickly become a whirlwind of activity. Knowing when and where decisions will be made and when people will be in attendance at specific meetings maintains the momentum of a project's most important tasks. Even as project members get distracted and sidelined by their many competing interests, their awareness of a meeting every Thursday morning, say at 10:00 a.m. (at which they must report on the status of their task to a group of peers and others), will encourage them to make time for their responsibilities.

Schedule everything related to the project. Note on the battle rhythm when information is due to you and when reports will be sent by you to the project stakeholders. Establishing standing meetings that drive a project, whether on a daily, weekly, or monthly schedule, maintains the project's momentum even when it might otherwise slow to a crawl due to vacations, distractions, or those days when you just don't feel like doing things. The battle rhythm will keep the project moving forward when people cannot, and it will lead you in step down the road of implementation.

For the Risk-Based Inspection System, we created and published a biweekly battle rhythm so that everyone was aware of when we would meet, what decisions would be made, and when they would be accountable to the group.

ENGAGE KEY STAKEHOLDERS

For any project to succeed, you need the buy-in of key stakeholders. This starts in the initial "collect, organize, and assess" phase, as discussed in chapter 1, but it's important to continue to engage these stakeholders as you continue through the project. There are different strategies you can use to do this.

DON'T RELY ON DATA ALONE

In chapter 2, I discussed how data is the lifeblood of project management, but it is important to note that for a variety of reasons, many government stakeholders who have done business a particular way for a long time will be suspicious of data and its insights.

At the fire department, for example, some resisted using data-driven computer programs to determine which buildings to inspect. Sometimes, what the computer spit out was not in line with the experience and expertise of fire chiefs; failed efforts to rely on data analysis in the past had led their operations astray. This needed to be considered. We built the system in a way that provided maximum flexibility and deferred to the wisdom of those doing the work. That meant that the system would never be "the truth" of what needed inspecting. Rather, departmental policy gave captains and chiefs the latitude to conduct the inspections they thought relevant, which could be added to the system. The system became an additional, albeit very robust tool in their arsenal of fire prevention with deference to leadership and their experience.

If we didn't engage the captains and chiefs and consider their valuable input, the project would not have been as successful.

GIVE A STARTING POINT

Often, stakeholders want to contribute, but they don't know where to begin. Give teams something to react to when getting them started. That is, make a draft of whatever product or document needs to be created.

In the case of the Risk-Based Inspection System, I struggled to get an overall rollout and training plan timeline from the team responsible for overseeing it until I created a draft of one and shared it with my contact. By creating a draft, I showed them what the project team was looking for and got the juices flowing for the training team to put one together and refine what I started for them.

USE FAMILIAR PRODUCTS AND TOOLS

The easier it is for stakeholders to engage in the project, the more likely they are to do so. For this reason, use familiar products, tools, and formats so your audience will be comfortable with what you produce.

For example, consultants to the project team provided a weekly status report that went through multiple refinements before the team settled on a format they liked. So, rather than reinventing the wheel, I used that format as a model for my own and obtained stakeholder buy-in much more easily.

USE BUREAUCRACY TO YOUR ADVANTAGE

Bureaucracy can be a great frustration, but you can also use it to your advantage.

Several times during this project, I needed key information or actions from individuals who did not report directly to me, and it was sometimes a challenge to obtain a response or get them to do the work the project needed. I would have to sit in my boss's office to explain why a particular task was stalled and that I needed a key piece of information or action from someone not on the project team. When we confronted these situations, he offered a tactic that I used from time to time when I really needed to nudge something along.

"Jeff, here's what I'm going to do," he said. "I'll send you an email asking for an update to the project. Forward that along to so-and-so, who will know that I'm asking for the information." The email took the pressure off me to nag someone for a response and put the accountability at a higher level. This powerful tool helped move items through the bureaucracy when things needed a little prodding.

DO A PILOT PROGRAM AND GET FEEDBACK

Pilots are a must for any size project at any time. There is always a way to test and rehearse ideas before committing resources to concepts or half-baked projects that are not ready for full implementation. This is similar to a minimum viable product as discussed in *The Lean Startup* by Eric Ries (2011), who understands that success is driven by starting small, refining, and scaling when ready.

Using a pilot was pivotal to the successful implementation of the Risk-Based Inspection System. During the entire technical build-out, the department's IT team wisely partnered with a fire operations battalion to test the new application and provide weekly feedback to the technology development team. When orders came to speed up the implementation timeline, we already had the benefit of stakeholder engagement and feedback. There was also a long list of requirements that were needed to make the application viable. With feedback from the pilot battalion, the team distilled the requirements to a list of must-haves before the application would be more broadly deployed. The idea was that the app needed certain features before we could start rolling it out, but the rollout would take a very long time (nine months in total was the plan). The nice-to-haves could be developed and the updates pushed after the rollout had commenced.

The training team oversaw the program to roll out the application, division by division, across the department. They designed the user guides, training, and curriculum and even went so far as to train super users who were available at the department's Building Inspections Safety

Program hotline. This was a group of fire officers who worked tours at the hotline and were trained in the software. They provided support to fire officers in the field who were using the application, answering questions in depth as to how the application interacted with operations and about the policies and procedures of the department in regard to building inspections. Thus, the project benefited from a pilot, from supporting materials for those who were learning the system, and from a hotline that users could call anytime to find support.

In this project, the fire officers were critical stakeholders who would ultimately use the application we were building in their day-to-day operations, so we pulled a representative from the user community into the project to represent the uniformed perspective on our weekly technical committee. The main representative to our project was a chief who commanded one of the battalions piloting the project and whose timely, consistent feedback paid dividends to our project's success. It may not always be feasible to have someone commit as much time to a project as he did to ours, but scheduling predictable times for stakeholders to give feedback is crucial to project success. Define and establish those feedback loops early in a project and use them to gain insight into the project along the path of implementation.

We made improvements to the application along the way

based on our stakeholders' feedback, and the pilot battalion immediately implemented and tested those changes. This allowed the project team to assess what was and was not absolutely critical in building the software and ensured that it was a ready product before it was rolled out citywide. Starting small allowed us to test our ideas, try them out, receive feedback, and revamp our plans before scaling up.

COMMUNICATE, COMMUNICATE, COMMUNICATE

Communication is key to keeping a project on track. Communicating regularly is critical to ensuring that all members of the project team are on the same page. Regularly pushing information, meeting with stakeholders, and ensuring that they're aware of concerns long before they become crises militates against sudden and unanticipated problems. Those will always arise, but many are preventable and can be managed well before they become urgent. The more proactive you are in your communication, the more time you save, and the more problems you avoid.

For the Risk-Based Inspection System, we communicated regularly with key stakeholders as well as stakeholders whom others would not necessarily consider an integral part of the project team. In our case, the city's Office of Management and Budget (OMB) was a critical partner in our project because they approved or denied spending related to it. These transactions could take a significant amount of time and could be slowed by OMB if they needed to request information from a project team. We met with them, at their location, once a month to update them from the dashboard. Because we proactively pushed information their way and regularly engaged with them, transactional decisions came with fewer follow-up questions. They already had the information! More than once, this proved invaluable in our ability to manage the project's budget and quickly move funds as needed from one project area to another. It also had the benefit of making our OMB partners feel like valued and important partners in our project, which they were.

To provide another example, we met with both the fire officers' and firefighters' unions to let them know what the project was and why we were doing it, as well as sending them regular updates. We did this long before we engaged the membership directly to ensure that we had the support of the unions, or at the very least, to ensure they were not surprised if and when their membership brought them questions or concerns. Establishing a relationship paved the path and skirted potential pitfalls when challenges arose and when we implemented the tool in the firehouses.

For effective, proactive communication, follow these tips.

PUSH INFORMATION

Information can be pushed or pulled. My experience in both city government and the military has proven beyond doubt that determining what your boss and overseers need to know and finding ways to provide that information before they ask for it (or even before they know they need it) goes a long way toward allaying the anxiety that comes to decision makers when they simply do not have critical information.

Sending regular reports, information, status updates, and the like to stakeholders not only limits people pestering you for information but also drives action around a project. People will not call you for information if they know that every Thursday at 4:00 p.m., for example, you will send a status report with the information they need. Similarly, regularly communicating a project's status creates a sense that the project is moving and brings attention and focus to it. Even if a project is stalled, decision makers will pay attention because week after week, there seems to be no movement updated in the status report. Consistently providing reports creates those conditions.

Create a report, newsletter, or other mechanism for sharing information on a consistent basis with key stakeholders. Do not wait for your stakeholder, boss, or client to request the information. Anticipate what they need and push it, and make the push regular and consistent. For example, I used the dashboard to push information to my project teams so the team became used to getting the information and knew when to expect it. That lessened the number of data requests I received as everyone knew when the biweekly report would come out.

KNOW WHAT INFORMATION YOUR BOSS NEEDS OR WANTS

Knowing what information your boss needs or wants is crucial to becoming valuable to your boss and taking things off their plate. Listen for the questions they ask frequently, understand whom they report to and what they are asked for, and maybe crawl into their heads and consider what data, reports, or information would help them do their jobs. Create a sample and share it with colleagues to get their input. Try to build something that creates understanding or knowledge. In the hierarchy of information, do not give only data; try to provide analysis in the data presentation to help your boss make sense of what you present. In other words, answer the "So what?" question of why the information is important and what it represents.

CREATE A PROJECT DASHBOARD

Creating a project dashboard is critical. It provides a snapshot of the health of a project and allows you, as the project manager, to easily push information to your key stakeholders. This will give them confidence in the health of the project and your management abilities and will enable them to identify and work on issues or concerns long before they become crises.

A project dashboard also helps you anticipate changes and prevent or prepare for issues. By tracking the project's administrative metrics and anticipating when resources will be used and at what rate, a project manager can determine whether the project is on track. If things are speeding up, adjustments can be made long before they become a significant problem. For example, one technical task in our project was slowing down because we lost a key member of the technical development staff. We compensated in terms of the timeline by having other staff work overtime, but that affected our budget. We knew that given our increased spending due to overtime, we would hit a budget shortfall in three months. Forecasting this early allowed us to coordinate with city hall and the OMB months in advance of the problem, which meant it never became a problem. Rather, it was something we saw could become a problem, and we nipped it in the bud long before it became more significant.

An additional benefit of using a dashboard is that it creates a record of the project's progress. Saving the dashboards allows you to return to them from time to time, if necessary, to better understand how the project is progressing. For instance, a metrics tracking sheet system can allow you to view in a snapshot the progress of key indicators throughout the life cycle of the project, revealing the highs and lows. Over time, this helps a project team anticipate resource shortfalls or other cyclical events that may not be anticipated early in the project's management. For example, if everyone takes vacations in August, you may need to determine how this will affect task completion as your resources will be constrained. Likewise, when the fiscal teams freeze payments due to year-end accounting procedures, planning to make budget modifications then is probably not ideal.

A PROJECT DASHBOARD EXAMPLE

A project dashboard was key to the Risk-Based Inspection System. All the project's attributes had to be monitored and communicated to its various stakeholders, so we immediately set to work to create a simple dashboard of key project variables. We pulled ideas from other departmental projects that city hall was also interested in and from which they were already receiving regular reports. We followed a similar format so that our project dashboard would be familiar to our intended audience.

On the dashboard, we wanted to highlight the project's health and draw attention to areas where we needed help from city hall to address an issue or concern. This dashboard tool was not meant to make everything on the project seem hunky-dory but to focus the energies of city hall where they could best serve the project. For example, if the timeline was slowing down due to staffing needs that required funding approval from the city's OMB (such as hiring a consultant skilled in the development of a particular component), we wanted city hall to be aware and to use its influence to expedite our approvals. In other words, although it was a tool geared to providing city hall with information, we also used it to focus on where we needed help.

We used a red, yellow, and green indicator system to highlight the health status of items such as project timeline, budget, scope, technical development, and training rollout. If the project was on time and on budget, these areas were highlighted in green. If an item required some level of attention, I highlighted it in yellow, and an urgent or critical item was highlighted in red. Note that I never sent a report in which anything highlighted in red was new to the audience; a red-level indicator meant that conversations and phone calls had already been made to inform decision makers that a critical component of the project needed immediate attention.

The dashboard also listed all the activities that had taken place in the previous reporting period and all those upcoming, making everyone who read the report aware of what actions the project team had taken and planned to take. We included any notes, issues, or concerns that needed to be highlighted for decision makers regarding the activities of the project team.

The most powerful tools for understanding the project's health were our project progress indicators.

These simple, highly focused tools contributed greatly to managing the overall success of the project for the entire duration of which we monitored and tracked these indicators. For each, we projected how many items would be completed each month, which allowed us to track whether the project was moving along as planned. This also allowed us to actively address issues with the project rather than reacting to them.

Each progress indicator included a projected value or target (where we thought we would be) and the actual status at that point in time. We listed the target as the denominator and the actual status at a given time period as the numerator. For example, we had thirteen technical items being developed, tested, and released before the entire application was fully implemented, and I knew from our detailed project plan the months in which each of those thirteen tasks would be completed. I looked across the year (in this case, January to November, when the project was due to be completed) and marked the number of the thirteen technical items that would be completed in each month. In January, we expected to have four items completed. We would not complete any others until March, when two more of the thirteen (or six total) were scheduled to be completed, and so on. As I prepared the dashboard in each of those months, I reported the total we had actually completed. In January, we completed three of the four tasks. However, we knew that there was a short delay for the fourth task, which was actually completed in February, when we reported four of four.

This tool became very helpful for budget tracking. We knew what our overall project budget was for the time remaining, and we projected how we would spend funds through each phase of the project. Our most significant cost was for the development staff, and we were able to determine how much we would spend to complete the technical tasks related to the items that were scheduled in each month of the project plan based on the hours needed to complete the assignments. This was not an exacting science but a means to give us indication—that is, a ball-park figure. I then calculated the overall spend down of our budget month over month and updated it. We started overspending in April and May, so I highlighted those months in yellow and red. When we saw in April that our spending was above expectations (our target), we alerted our stakeholders, including the OMB. As a result, we devised solutions to the problem and got everyone on board. When we overspent in May, it was not alarming because everyone was tracking. Given the urgent nature of the project and the marching orders from our commissioner and city hall, we continued to advance the project according to the timeline.

The project progress indicators offered places for management to ask critical questions, such as: If we were overspending the project budget, why was that? Were we asking our team to work overtime to meet the technical development schedule? Did something else come up? If we were underspending, why was that? Did someone have to take an emergency leave, and would that impact the project's momentum?

The dashboard was a vital element of project communication, and I found that sending it on a recurring, consistent basis lessened the early barrage of questions that came from city hall on a frequent basis. As they became used to the reporting format and gained confidence that the project was moving on the planned timeline and that changes were dealt with and communicated immediately, the overseers outside our agency found less need to call to extract information from us.

MAKING AN IMPACT

The project team was a talented group of individuals, all dedicated to changing business processes related to building inspections in NYC. We believed that these changes would equip fire officers with a powerful tool for making important decisions in their day-to-day operations. We closed this phase of the project at a press conference with our commissioner and Mayor Bloomberg, announcing the changes at a firehouse.

It was very rewarding to be part of a project that could save lives or at least make it easier for firefighters to do their jobs. Even better, the FDNY recognized our entire project team at a ceremony later that year, awarding the team the FDNY Administrative Medal, the department's highest civilian award, for the work we did on this important project.

KEY TAKEAWAYS

I learned a number of critical lessons about implementing a complicated project that had the attention of key, high-level leadership (e.g., our commissioner and city hall). Several factors made the difference in our ability to deliver on time and to meet the diverse expectations of our stakeholders.

Creating a detailed project plan was critical to keeping

everyone on task and on the same page. Then, establishing the governance of the project, along with a battle rhythm, kept the project moving forward.

Next, it's important to find a way to rehearse and test concepts prior to full implementation. There are dozens of ways to conduct a pilot or rehearsal, and it is an absolute must. In this instance, we had support from a battalion that provided regular feedback throughout the entire development and implementation process. Having that regular interaction was absolutely invaluable not only for building and testing a functional tool but also for getting buy-in from the uniformed side of the agency. Find a way to test your product, concept, and ideas before fully implementing them. If you can do it through preexisting channels, all the better.

Finally, be sure to communicate proactively. Information is obtained either through a push or a pull. I find that pushing information is usually better for managing a project or program. A project dashboard is a great tool for this. In this project, we engaged leadership early and often, pushing information in a regular, consistent, and recurring manner to keep everyone informed. We met regularly and proactively with key stakeholders before they had questions or concerns. This helped us get out in front of potential problems.

As you stay on the path of the project, your next step is to begin measuring your progress. (See graphic 4.3 for an example of a Project Progress Indicator Tracking Tool.)

Figure 4.3: Sample Project Progress Indicators Tracking Tool

INDICATOR (Actual/Target)	JAN	FEB	MAR	APR	MAY	JUN	JUL	AUG	SEP	OCT	NOV
Number of tasks completed (total: 13)	3/4	4/4	4/4	6/6	7/7	7/7	/8	/8	/11	/11	/13
Percentage of technical development completed	26	35	40/39	41/41	45/45	/50	/55	/59	/75	/85	/100
Total number of defects tracked	17	20	27	28	*	11					
Total number of defects corrected (required for rollout)	3	9/4	11/5	11/5	*	2					
Number of pilot battalions using RBIS	5/5	8/5	11/11	11/11	11/11	11/11	11/11	11/11	11/11	11/11	11/11
Number of battalions using RBIS											
Number of officers trained											
Percentage of battalions/officers trained											
Percentage of budget liquidated	–	52	53	54	55	56					
Percentage of funds invoiced	15	21	30	37/26	44/34	/43	/51	/59			
Percentage of "QA" funds invoiced	0	5	11	18/14	24/23	/33	/42	/52			

Requires notification of Steering Committee / Management team attention to address.

Requires notification of Steering Committee / Urgent, requires immediate Steering Committee attention to address.

CHAPTER 5

TRACK AND SHARE YOUR PROGRESS

To keep your project moving forward, track the most important metrics, and share the progress. This builds and keeps your momentum.

"If you don't collect any metrics, you're flying blind. If you collect and focus on too many, they may be obstructing your field of view."

—SCOTT M. GRAFFIUS

In 2014, the City of New York commenced a major initiative to end pedestrian fatalities from vehicular traffic by 2024, known as Vision Zero (Nonko 2019). As detailed in the action plan, "Today in New York, approximately 4,000 New Yorkers are seriously injured and more than

250 are killed each year in traffic crashes. Being struck by a vehicle is the leading cause of injury-related death for children under 14, and the second leading cause for seniors. On average, vehicles seriously injure or kill a New Yorker every two hours" (City of New York 2014, 7). These were serious statistics and deserved the city's attention. The mayor formed a task force of multiple city agencies, community organizations, and businesses that came together to identify ways to address the issue. Based on a Swedish model to make streets safer for pedestrians, Vision Zero was gaining traction in the United States, starting in NYC (Center for Active Design n.d.). The tenets of the program sought to improve pedestrian street safety through street design techniques and street calming measures.

At the time, I was the deputy commissioner of policy and external affairs at the NYC TLC. Given that TLC licensed and regulated over 140,000 drivers and over 80,000 vehicles (and growing) of yellow taxis and for-hire vehicles for companies such as Uber and Lyft, we were a critical partner in this effort. The TLC's role was to create training and outreach programs to educate drivers and the companies who hire them and to ensure they understood the rules of the road and how to be safe drivers.

As part of our contribution to the Vision Zero task force, the TLC produced a very powerful video called *Drive like Your Family Lives Here* that became central to the outreach and education program (NYC Taxi and Limousine Commission 2015). It showcased a few families of pedestrian victims of vehicular traffic, who told their heartbreaking stories. It was a stark reminder that the choices a driver makes matter. It also brought a very human element to the initiative by reminding us that there were real people behind the statistics.

Vision Zero was a massive initiative that pulled in dozens of project members from various city agencies and community organizations. From the get-go, the project established a clear objective and the means that each agency would employ to move the city to the end point: zero pedestrian fatalities. Deciding what to measure to achieve that objective was the hard part, but with the right people at the table, the task force was able to identify all the interventions the city would take to address speeding, red light violations, and unsafe driving practices. Building upon the concepts of street design, NYC coupled that focus with additional measures to educate the public about the impacts of unsafe driving, and to step up enforcement. The project team at city hall created a scorecard to track all of these measures on a regular and consistent basis. Establishing the scorecard, measuring progress, and making the results publicly available were all important components of the initiative.

ESTABLISH YOUR METRICS EARLY

It is important to set the metrics of a project/program early in its life cycle. I had the privilege of being part of the Bloomberg administration in which data were a ubiquitous component of decision making. In most cases, metrics were identified when a project commenced, which allowed us to go into the project knowing what data to collect, what needed to be measured, and how those data would translate into whether the project proved successful.

We thought through the key performance indicators (KPIs) for each project and vetted them through the project's steering committee to ensure buy-in from all the stakeholders. Always, particularly when a project involved multiple city agencies (diverse organizations with roles in a project or program), we created a metrics committee that identified the KPIs, what constituted success, and how the data would be collected and reported. Vision Zero, among the first initiatives of the de Blasio administration, followed a similar path for establishing metrics early.

Conversely, I have witnessed projects that failed to perform very well. Always, always, always, the absence of clear, definitive metrics from the get-go leads to confusion as to what the project is supposed to accomplish and how the project is performing in driving toward the specific metrics. It also increases public scrutiny of the project given the apparent lack of transparency. Having a clear set of collaboratively established KPIs keeps everyone on the same page, makes it easy to communicate the health and status of a project internally and externally, and gives the team insight into whether they are achieving the intended results or need to correct their course.

Knowing the metrics early also prevents scope creep (i.e., the tendency of a project to take on new and ever different tasks). Even when you face scope creep, basing your project's success or end state on specific, measurable outcomes allows you to drive a stake in the ground and claim victory. You must know what that measure is from the beginning of the project. Chart its course down to completion and celebrate when you hit the mark. This allows for a clean end to the major efforts related to the project, even if some minor items remain to be closed out.

DETERMINE KEY PERFORMANCE METRICS

Determining your key performance metrics is vital to measuring the progress of your action plan. In addition to establishing these metrics early in the process, you want to be thoughtful in what you choose to measure. To determine your key performance metrics, look at your start point, your desired end point, and the detailed plan you've created to get you from point A to point B. Within that plan, identify the critical tasks and milestones—the ones that must be accomplished—and then determine which metrics will measure your progress in those tasks. Another approach is to think about the action items that will lead to the end state. What are those daily action items that we can measure, that we believe will lead us to our objective? Then measure those actions. That is a performance indicator. The most important among those performance indicators are KPIs.

My team always creates an annual strategic plan with a starting point that defines where we want to take a project or program in a specific year. With those objectives defined and the action plan spelled out, we identified the tasks that have to be accomplished and the milestones that must be reached to move the team from point A to point B. These measures focus the team on the most important items. We review them every week at a team huddle to ensure that the crucial items are given attention and not lost in the whirlwind of daily distractions. These measures are vital metrics—that is, the most important things that must be accomplished to drive toward the objective.

In Vision Zero, each participating city agency had a list of interventions that they could use to improve the safety of pedestrians using the city's streets. Perhaps improved street design could ensure that the public was safe when crossing busy intersections. Maybe curve-outs at crosswalks or speed bumps at high-traffic, high-pedestrian intersections would help. Better signage and reduced speed limits could help, as could bike lanes separated from vehicular traffic. The city could also do outreach to educate the public on the program, on how to be a better and safer driver, and on how to be careful as a pedestrian on NYC's busy streets. These all were part of a massive list of methods the city was employing to improve the safety of streets. To measure the different agencies' progress toward their identified interventions, the city measured a number of KPIs. At TLC, for example, we had education and outreach programs, and one of our KPIs was the number of drivers who attended a Vision Zero education event. Increasing this number was one among many actions that we believed would contribute to moving the city to zero fatalities. Other KPIs across the city included the number of Vision Zero-related driver summonses given by the NYPD and the TLC, the number of miles of bike lanes installed, the number of speed bumps installed across the city, and the number of city employees who had completed a defensive driving course. By measuring all these KPIs, the city could make sure we were on track to achieving our overall goal.

LEAD AND LAG METRICS

Lead and lag metrics are another approach to measuring a project's progress and are crucial to keeping you on the right path. Lead metrics, according to the *4 Disciplines of Execution*, are those that impact a lag metric (McChesney,

Covey, and Huling 2012), and a lag metric is what you are trying to achieve.

It's important to track both lead and lag metrics. Think about it in terms of weight loss. The lag metric would be the thing you want to improve—such as your overall body weight, your body fat percentage, or body mass index. If all you do is measure your lag metric every day, without adjusting and measuring the daily activities that will improve your lag metric, nothing will change. The lead metrics are the things you will do to impact the lag. For example, perhaps you measure your daily step count or the number of workouts you do, or you count your calories and cap it at a certain daily target. If you get these things right, the lag metric will naturally improve over time. If it doesn't, you may need to rethink your actions or determine if you are correctly measuring your lead metrics.

Policy strategy and interventions work in the same way. In Vision Zero, the lag metric was simple and straightforward: zero pedestrian traffic fatalities in NYC by 2024. There were numerous lead metrics that impacted this lag metric. For example, when drivers break the rules, stricter enforcement at traffic signals and pedestrian crosswalks ensures that they face consequences. Thus, the number of summonses given for infractions at traffic signals functions as a lead metric. All the tools that could lower pedestrian fatalities closer to zero (improved street design, education, etc.) were the basis for the city's lead metrics. The task then became to track these improvements and interventions to see how they impacted overall traffic fatalities. In this project, like in many, the solution was not a single intervention but several together that produced the intended results. To the manager of such a project, knowing the overall goal and tracking the number of interventions implemented is critical to understanding how the policies and actions of city government can directly impact the lag goal.

For your project, if you've clearly defined your end point, the ultimate outcome you are trying to achieve is the lag metric. Identify how to measure it, which may not always be easy to do. The important thing is to identify elements of your project that are measurable that you believe you can impact by increasing or decreasing action items. These are your lead metrics. Measure those action items and set targets for how much you want them to change and over what period of time. Increase? Decrease? Measure, record those items, and over time observe how they impact your lag metric. If there seems to be limited change, you may need to revisit your lead metrics or identify new action items altogether.

SHARE YOUR PROGRESS

Most project managers understand the importance of

sharing progress with key stakeholders, but they don't always share their progress publicly. When you're working in the public sector, though, the public is one of your key stakeholders.

Vision Zero is a great example of this because it is a project that directly and clearly impacts the public. Accordingly, the city government has published a number of public reports that include Vision Zero data. Vision Zero also has its own website where the public can view the scorecard and the data for the project. There are also links to Vision Zero-related data, reports, and research. And there is an interactive map that allows users to view traffic crashes, street design measures in place, and established speed limits on each city street.

Open data is ubiquitous today, but this was not always so, and there always seem to be barriers to releasing data in the public sector. I believe it is incredibly important to put data out there. Sharing data creates trust with the public, allows them to understand what government is doing and how it is performing, and allows for fact-checking of governmental entities in their public statements. Even though releasing data may lead to public scrutiny, it is part of governing in a democratic system. Open, transparent, responsible government requires accountability, and open data is one factor that can help strengthen those things. Do it in thoughtful, disciplined ways, but get it out.

At the NYC TLC, for example, we created a Data and Technology Advisory Team of academics and industry experts to help us learn to release data responsibly. We released billions of data records from companies such as Uber and Lyft so the public could do their own analysis and make sense of that changing industry. We tied the public release of data to hackathons during my time at both the TLC and the FDNY, encouraging community interaction with our data and policy teams. Making such inroads with data consumers builds bridges and provides insights into data and policy.

Releasing raw data in this way can be powerful, but especially when you want to share your progress, be thoughtful in how you present the data. According to statistician Edward Tufte, "There are two goals when presenting data: convey your story and establish credibility." Once data is collected, organized, structured, and understood in terms of how it is created, it tells us a story. It is imperative to learn the skills of using infographics, maps, charts, dashboards, and other graphics to build a compelling story, to evoke emotion, or to make the data pop, sing, shout, or enrage. Providing one place for the public to gain access and insight into the project, like the Vision Zero website, also helps tell the story of the work being done. If feasible, get out and tell your story. This is one of the most engaging ways to share your project. If you've led a project in government, attend conferences or seminars and ask to be a presenter. Or look for awards that you can apply to, particularly if your project was innovative. Several academic institutions give awards and recognition to governments that create change.

As you tell your story, remember to always be truthful with data; the idea is to create understanding and wisdom. To do that, the data must tell a story that sticks with your audience, but if you distort or twist facts for the sake of the story, you will undercut your credibility. Balance story and credibility, and you will bring immeasurable value to your organization.

MAKING AN IMPACT

Vision Zero has saved lives. Total fatalities decreased from 2015 to 2018. Although there was a slight uptick in 2019, it was the second lowest year of total fatalities on record (from 2001 to 2020). There was also a considerable drop in fatalities at key intersections. All in all, this was important work.

However, this wasn't the only impact. As a result of convening a task force of leaders from government, community organizations, and businesses, this project has contributed to an overall focus on improving the safety and quality of life of pedestrians who rely on the city's streets, sidewalks, and public spaces to commute and recreate. Moreover, relationships now exist to build on this work for years to come. Keeping score, and communicating a project well to the public, has other benefits as well. In this case, NYC has made great strides to change how the city thinks about street design and how pedestrians, cyclists, drivers, and others use the streets. Bringing government agencies and community leaders to the table to focus on one initiative gives those leaders an opportunity to foster relationships. Initiatives will ultimately birth new programs, projects, and initiatives that will lead to further change.

The most important thing to remember, and what *Drive like Your Family Lives Here* reminds us, is that public policy impacts very real people. Hearing the stories of those who lost a family member due to an unavoidable traffic crash gives the initiative purpose. The stories make the issue very real and very personal. Measuring the progress of key indicators to move an initiative toward the objective isn't about statistics—it's about making an impact to improve people's lives. In the case of Vision Zero, to save lives.

KEY TAKEAWAYS

Making an impact starts with knowing what you want to accomplish, measuring the indicators that will ensure you get there, keeping score regularly and consistently, fine-tuning and refining as necessary, and seeing the momentum build as you move toward your objective.

Defining the objective and measuring the right things in the right ways matters. Start with the metrics in mind, from the get-go. Do it right away. Do not pass go. Do not collect $200. Establishing the metrics early will bring clarity and transparency to your projects.

Choose to measure the lead metrics—that is, the team's actions that take place each and every day that you believe will impact the lag metric, the thing you are trying to achieve.

And be clear and up front about your data. Provide it publicly and in ways that the public can easily access it and understand it.

CHAPTER 6

CLOSE THE LOOP

Go the extra step and close out your projects and programs, recognize your team, and record what you've learned along the way.

"An organization's ability to learn, and translate that learning into action rapidly, is the ultimate competitive advantage."

—JACK WELCH

We scurried across Broadway from our office building, through the security gate, and into the main entrance of city hall. I was eager for this meeting. Members of my office had recently completed the build of a 311 call center application that would enable NYC residents to report a variety of quality-of-life concerns to the city by interfacing with a simple app on their smartphones. Smartphones were still relatively new, and the city of New York deploying its own app to increase access to city services was an innovative concept. We were on our way to give a presentation to the mayor on a prototype of the app that our team had put together to determine whether the mayor wanted to include it in a series of technology innovations in city government he was set to announce as part of his Connected City Initiative.

The 311 line was among Mayor Bloomberg's marquee accomplishments as mayor. A call center designed to give citizens access to nonemergency city services, 311 was proving to be wildly popular, and it remains so almost twenty years later. It gave citizens the ability to call a single number to access city services in any language at any time of the day or night. The call center handles twenty million calls each year, connecting citizens with dozens of city services from notifying the city of a pothole to reporting a lost wallet in the back of a cab to complaining about that loud party upstairs from your apartment. Although it was a significant innovation in its own right, the mayor also wanted to expand the means by which people could connect with the call center and have their requests routed to the appropriate city agency for response.

My team was part of the project that designed the application. We worked with the city's technology gurus to build and deploy the application on an ambitious timeline set by city hall. At the time, I was a policy analyst in the Mayor's Office of Operations, Project Management Group. A few of us had been brought on to help steer the project to completion by the impending deadline, and we had done it. Through countless meetings, late nights, and the use of data to help us determine which conditions were most widely reported to 311 by New Yorkers, we created a simple app that allowed citizens to push information to the 311 call center for a city response. Each time a user interacted with the application, a service request (SR) was created and routed to the city agency responsible for responding to the SR. For example, if citizens wanted to report a pothole, they could enter some basic information, such as its location and related details; they could also snap a picture and attach it to the request. This SR would go through the app into the 311 SR database and make its way to the NYC Department of Transportation, where it would be assessed and fixed as appropriate.

When the deadline for creating the application was fast approaching, we pulled various experts to the table to build a pilot application. We then tested the app multiple times, wanting to work out all the kinks before we finalized it and made it available on the Apple store and in the Android market. We now had a prototype we were proud of, and we were excited to show the mayor what we had created and help the team prepare for the public release.

We'd put in the hours and done all the hard work needed to bring this project to fruition. All that was left was to close the loop: nail the final presentation, celebrate the project's completion, and document everything we'd learned.

TAKE RESPONSIBILITY FOR CLOSING THE LOOP

As the leader or project manager of a project or program, the responsibility for closing the loop falls on you. It's one of your most important responsibilities. You and your team can do incredible work for months, but if you slip up at this crucial stage of the project, it won't matter.

One of the toughest lessons I ever learned was during an intense military training exercise at the army's National Training Center (NTC) in Fort Irwin, California. Here, units go through an intensive training scenario, a Combat Readiness Center, that is built to replicate combat. In these experiences, the pressure is certainly on. The exercise is meant to stress people and organizations to such an extent that their weaknesses readily become apparent and can therefore be fixed.

During our unit's experience and before we entered the "box," the infamous location where the training takes place, my battalion commander had to give a daily update to the commander of the NTC, who wanted stats to record the progress of the unit in completing various aspects of the training. One of my tasks was to compile these data on a daily basis, roll them up into a PowerPoint slide, and submit it to our next higher headquarters' staff, who compiled the data from multiple battalions. One issue was that these data were incredibly difficult to obtain, make sense of, and reconcile.

In one such daily roll-up, I stayed up much later than everyone else to finish compiling our numbers. In the wee hours of the night, I finally finished, burned the PowerPoint slide to a CD, and traipsed across the area where our tents were located to turn in the slide for my commander's 0700 briefing to the commanding general. Passing the CD off to the staff, I thanked them for the support before heading to my cot in one of the barrack areas.

When our commander attended the briefing, he stood up before the group to give his report only to find that the numbers were not up to date, though everyone else's were. This was completely unacceptable in such an environment, where the intensity and focus on training must be precise and error-free. I had failed to close the loop to ensure that the updated slide was actually inputted into the presentation. I had off-handed the CD to a staff member who was responsible for compiling the various units' slides, but I had not closed the loop by confirming that he actually copied over our updated data.

Needless to say, my commander was not at all happy, and in his anger he called me out in front of my peers in our unit's morning meeting for failing to close the loop. This very painful experience has stayed with me all these years.

A job is not complete until you've verified that the loop is closed and everything is situated as it should be. Take the extra step to ensure that the updates are made. Check and double-check to ensure everything is complete. Taking a few extra minutes to do this would have saved significant pain and embarrassment to my commander and our unit.

As the leader or project manager of a project or program, you own it. You are responsible for everything the project team does or fails to do. This is a big responsibility. You ensure that everything has met the standard and meets the expectation of the project's client. Take the time to review documents, reports, tasks, and anything that you delegated to someone else. Make sure that what was done or delivered meets the expectation you have for quality, for intent, and for what your boss is ultimately looking for. You are the only person within the group who can perform this vital function as the project leader. Go look at the things that you expect to be accomplished. Sit with project members as they work on their tasks. See how they are progressing. Offer guidance along the path to ensure that the final product is not the first time you see what you asked for.

NAIL THE FINAL PRESENTATION

Generally, closing the loop and finalizing a project requires a presentation of the work that was done. A presentation with a final report to the principals (or client) who requested the project is a common approach.

Our final presentation for the 311 app took place in the Blue Room at city hall, the iconic press room where mayors give press briefings and conduct other ceremonial business. The setup that day included a large TV screen and a place for the mayor to sit. The team had rehearsed what we were going to say multiple times and had just as many times tested the prototype that we would show the mayor. This was a no-fail mission, and we wanted the mayor to be proud of what we had built in hopes that it would make the cut for his public announcement.

Given our preparation, the demonstration went off without a hitch, and the mayor seemed very pleased. After asking some detailed questions about how it worked and who on the team had contributed to building it, he thanked us and left the room.

We did not know yet whether it would be part of his announcement, but thanks to our preparation, we had nailed the final presentation.

TAKE TIME TO CELEBRATE AND RECOGNIZE THE TEAM'S HARD WORK

When a project finishes, take the time for a "hail and fare-well" moment. Celebrate the success, recognize all that you and the team have accomplished, and say goodbye to the project before embarking on the next one.

Particularly in the public sector, where leaders are limited in how they can reward their employees, they must rely on other ways to honor the hard work of their teams and celebrate them when they've accomplished their goals. Whether a large-scale event that includes the principal (in our case, the mayor of NYC) or something like a pizza party or simply a sincere thank-you card, marking milestones and accomplishments is important. Recognize the team and its hard work. Take time to highlight these moments!

Being able to celebrate employees and their service is one of the best and rarest pleasures of being on a team, and these occasions don't have to be big or unwieldy. Even a team of a couple of people can take time out to recognize each other, formally or informally. Here are some strategies you can use, both big and small.

A CLOSING EVENT

The best of the final presentations I've participated in

included a recognition program at the end—a reception or other such small event.

Events mark the end of a project or wrap it all up and present it to the client (in this case, the mayor was our client, and the public was his). Pulling together an event that shares what we created with those we serve is critical for closing the loop on a project, bringing it full circle. It not only publicizes what was created but also serves as a milestone for the project team that worked hard to finish a project and deserves to be part of something that marks its completion on the calendar, a moment to acknowledge that something was created that did not exist before.

A reception is always welcome, and I have often splurged personal funds on coffee, bagels, and donuts or a pizza party, anything that allows people to connect in a way slightly different from that of the workday. Such small events bring people together, allow the team to engage with coworkers in a setting that isn't about deadlines or work projects, and enables esprit de corps and comradery to take root and thrive. They give a celebratory feel to the project and make it feel complete, letting you close out a chapter and usher in a new one (or say goodbye to team members and welcome new ones).

CLOSEOUT EMAIL

After the final presentation, I also find it particularly help-ful to send a closeout email or memo to all the project's stakeholders. In this, you can thank the principals, proj-ect team, and others who dedicated significant time and resources to the project. You can also point to what was accomplished and how far the project team came on a particular topic or issue. Whenever I put such documents or emails together, I am surprised at how far the journey was from point A to point B. Progress is easily overlooked in day-to-day project management, but when you take a few brief moments to step back and look, it becomes more readily apparent how much you were able to accomplish.

CERTIFICATES AND THANK-YOUS

Two very simple methods to recognize people that do not demand a big investment are certificates and formal thank-yous.

For certificates, create something nice, frame it for the recipient, and have it signed by the most senior person on the team. Even better, get the certificates signed by higher-ups. This can be kept and cherished by employees or at least be put in their employment files for the record.

For formal thank-yous, you could recognize key team members publicly (in front of the project team or the larger organization) or send handwritten thank-you notes (do not minimize the importance and significance of something as simple as a handwritten thank-you. They are extremely powerful and, oh, so rare!).

These strategies don't require a whole heck of a lot of effort, but they go a long way toward making people feel valued and that they contributed to a team. The certificates and awards I have received in my life are very meaningful, reminding me how persistently I have trudged to get things done.

AWARDS CEREMONY

For some reason, in many organizations, particularly in the public sector, there seems to be little appetite for recognizing people in a formal way, but formal awards ceremonies can go a long way.

I am very proud that, in my career, I've gotten to thank public servants for the work they do every day. During my time in the Mayor's Office of Operations, Mayor Bloomberg signed Executive Order 115, which established a customer service office on our team to create customer service standards across city agencies. Our focus was developing and supporting initiatives aimed at improving the relationships between city government and those interacting with the city for services. The overall goal being to improve the customer service of NYC government. The office was a place where we could share leading practices and coordinate improvements across service delivery methods and organizations.

The program included creating an awards and recognition program to honor frontline customer service staff. Each city agency nominated one person to be recognized at a reception at city hall. On the day of the event, the honorees arrived with their agency sponsors, and some of them brought their spouses, crowding the room with approximately one hundred people. The mayor had agreed to attend the reception—a surprise for the honorees.

The mayor strode into the Governor's Room, a long narrow room at the front of city hall's second floor that overlooks City Hall Park, and took his place at a small lectern set up at the end of the room for the reception. Everyone gathered around. He thanked the honorees for what they did every day and reminded them that they made a difference in the lives of ordinary New Yorkers. After his remarks, he posed for an individual photo with each of the forty honorees while they held their awards. The gesture meant an incredible amount to the honorees, who may never have even met the mayor, let alone posed for a one-on-one photo with him. It was a touching tribute, and I could tell that people were moved by the time he took with them. Indeed, to this day, I treasure a photo with the mayor taken at a staff event that he hosted at Gracie Mansion. I was one of hundreds of people in attendance, yet he patiently posed for photos with everyone. A couple of weeks later, an 8″ × 10″ glossy photo of the attendee with the mayor arrived in the mail.

I recently had the distinct pleasure of attending this event again for one of my own employees this past year, which marked its tenth anniversary.

DOCUMENT WHAT YOU'VE ACCOMPLISHED

After you've nailed the final presentation and taken the time to celebrate, to finish closing the loop on your projects, you must document what you accomplished. Please, please, please document your project, findings, report, and all the materials. In more instances than not, I have found that governmental organizations neglect the documentation of projects/programs, procedures, and so forth. Collecting those items at the end of a project and archiving them in a way that facilitates future access and review is vital. Such documentation is also a good way to archive the history of your projects, which will help you at other points in your career.

Here are two strategies to help you document what worked and what didn't, what needs improvement, and how the organization can make changes moving forward.

One of the more important tools for creating a culture of learning and performance improvement is the after-action review (AAR). This tool may be known by other names or exist in various formats, but they all drive toward the same end (a postmortem, lessons learned, etc.). The AAR aims to capture what went well in a project/program and what needs to improve. There are many ways to do this, ranging from informal to formal. In the army, we often called an informal AAR a "hot wash," which essentially describes a team coming together and discussing what went well (*sustains*) and what needed improvement (*improves*). A good approach is to ensure that the participants comment on what they could have done better or differently to improve outcomes in their individual roles and on what they did that worked well.

More formal AARs are facilitated (by the project manager or an outsider familiar with the project) and focus on the measures of success that governed the project. Here, again, the team should focus on sustains and improves, but the AAR may focus not only on the individuals in the project but also on how the project was managed overall, with discussion of sustains and improves in topic areas, such as the project's budget, stakeholder engagement, timeline, scope, final products, governance, outputs, and client satisfaction.

LESSONS-LEARNED ANALYSIS

Like AARs, lessons learned provides an opportunity to create a library of experiences that shape an organization and allow it to learn. Think of a lessons-learned library as a collection of the key takeaways from assessments conducted, AARs, leading practices, and so on. Anytime an organization recognizes success with a certain method or practice, it should capitalize on that learning by documenting it and making it easily accessible for future reference. In the book *Principles*, Ray Dalio (2017) urges leaders at all levels in an organization to consider documenting what they learn and the principles by which they operate. Similarly, documenting things that allow an organization to achieve results is absolutely crucial to maintaining long-term momentum.

MAKING AN IMPACT

Closing the loop is one of the most rewarding parts of the job because it's where you get to feel your impact.

For the 311 app, after our meeting with the mayor, we received questions from the speech writing and press teams, a good indication that it would be included in his public announcement. Being well prepared, we had already laid out draft talking points about the application that we thought the mayor should touch on. His team took a look at the draft and applied some pizzazz to make it really shine. As the project manager, I was now supporting the city hall team to wrap this up in a nice package for public release.

The announcement would be among other items that the mayor was touting as the city made strides to make city government more accessible, transparent, and accountable to all New Yorkers.[3] The tools that were being built were part of that effort and were meant to give even more New Yorkers streamlined ways to access city services.

The Mayor's Office held a press conference and issued a press release on October 1, 2009. "Starting today, New Yorkers can submit select quality-of-life complaints—with an option to attach pictures—to 311 via their iPhones. New Yorkers are already able to report complaints to 311 through mobile web browsers. The new, free iPhone application will streamline the process by allowing New Yorkers to report complaints to 311 using a program that identifies the user, determines the specific location of the condition reported using GPS technology, and allows easy uploads of photos. Going forward, this functionality will be expanded to other mobile phones, and enhanced so that any New Yorker can check the status of previously reported issues" (NYC.gov 2009).

---

3   Our app is not to be confused with another app that came several years later, which was not as well received publicly as the application we created in 2009.

Bringing a project from concept to prototype to life inspires an amazing feeling. Closing the project with something like a mayoral announcement stands as a high point in the life of a public servant. Being in the room when the mayor makes a decision or asks a question—seeing behind the scenes—that is the romance of being part of government. Having the chief make a presentation or give a speech that touts something you helped build is a remarkable way to close out a project and mark a milestone. Public servants receive little fanfare for their work, and there is no end-of-year bonus. The satisfaction comes from the work itself and from those moments when you get to be part of something bigger than yourself.

KEY TAKEAWAYS

Closing the loop of a project, program, or initiative means sizing up the problem, showing the success criteria, and tying up loose ends.

The final presentation is critical, but it's not the end of the project. After presenting your final findings, it's time to pay tribute to the team. This is particularly critical in the public sector, where opportunities to award and recognize those who go above and beyond are rare indeed.

After that, the final step of closing the loop means ensuring that the project is documented, recorded, and archived in a way that manages the knowledge. The end of a project or program (or moving it from one phase to another) should include an after-action review of lessons learned to identify what worked and what didn't, what needs improvement, and how the organization can make changes moving forward. This ensures that an organization becomes a learning community.

You now know the full process to take a project to completion:

1. Know where you are.
2. Define where you want to go.
3. Plan the route.
4. Stay on the path.
5. Track and share your progress.
6. Close the loop.

In the second part of the book, I will guide you through some of the common challenges you're likely to face, starting with how to build a team.

PART II

COMMON CHALLENGES

"The pessimist complains about the wind. The optimist expects it to change. The leader adjusts the sails."

—JOHN MAXWELL

"The...thing you can do to make your agency a more interesting place to work and consequently less bureaucratic is to enable those under you to feel they control their own areas of work. In this way they acquire a sense of ownership in what gets done and how they do it."

—KENNETH ASHWORTH

CHAPTER 7

HIGH-IMPACT TEAMS

Building and structuring teams is an important element of any successful project. This chapter explores building and focusing your project team to achieve results.

"Talent wins games, but teamwork and intelligence win championships."

—MICHAEL JORDAN

The commissioner slammed his hand on the table in excitement, exclaiming, "Get it done today!"

We sat in the commissioner's conference room, my boss and I directly across from him. The afternoon sunlight streamed into the room. We had just briefed him on the design to build an analytics unit at the FDNY. As part of a citywide effort to create data analysis capacity across city agencies, we had been asked by city hall to create a team emulating the Mayor's Office of Data Analytics (MODA). Once called the Mayor's Geek Squad by *The New York Times* (Feuer 2013), this team of savvy number crunchers, under the leadership of Michael Flowers, was using data from multiple sources to combat some of the city's most perplexing problems. It was a team of smart guys and gals with economics degrees who were hired to dig into the city's data coffers and apply big data insights to everyday NYC problems.

I was in my second year at the FDNY and had recently been promoted to Assistant Commissioner of Management Initiatives. My purview included management analysis and planning (MAP), grant monitoring (mainly homeland security grants of nearly $150 million), and internal auditing. MAP was responsible for creating response-time reports and using the data to support policy changes within the department.

Recently, I had been approached by a member of the city hall team who told me that they wanted to duplicate the MODA model across city agencies and that the FDNY was a solid place to start. First, because we had a number of data projects that required interagency coordination and would benefit from a team of data geniuses. Second, because we were implementing the Risk-Based Inspection System (RBIS), an inspection program for FDNY fire companies that conducted building inspections throughout the city. RBIS, discussed in chapter 4, was designed to use a risk model to score every building in NYC that the FDNY inspected and to identify those most at risk of a fire or other life safety event. This would require a data team to design and code the risk model, and we could either hire an external vendor to do that, or we could build a team to do it internally.

When we discussed the plan with the commissioner, we had his full support. From my perspective, he seemed to know how important it was to build analytical capacity at the agency, and he appreciated the need to have internal support for our own agency's most complex data questions. Like MODA, we would start small with eager, smart guys and gals who would dive headfirst into the city's data troves to see how we could leverage data to optimize resource allocation and inform decision making—in essence, to make us smarter.

Getting approval to build the team was only step one. From there, we had to design the team under the constraints of the civil service process, attract the right talent, and establish the team's value to the entire organization.

DESIGNING THE TEAM

To begin, I reached out to Flowers and asked whether we

could discuss in detail how to put a plan together and move it forward. On the day of our meeting, I traveled to the city's municipal building, a large Romanesque edifice that sits across from city hall and houses a number of city offices and agencies. The data team had a bullpen there and invited me in to sit with them at a small conference table in the center of the office. Flowers introduced me to his team members. One stood at his stand-up desk, another sat on a medicine ball. Not typical of city government offices.

I joined them at the table, and we discussed what we would try to do at the FDNY, starting with a discussion of team structure. They suggested a team of three to four data scientists (we would call them analysts), all reporting to a manager or director. This structure made sense for our team. We had four lines to create the unit (i.e., the head count that was established for hiring). They provided me with the job descriptions they had used to hire their team, which I refined for our positions. However, we faced a significant hurdle—we had to work under civil service constraints.

For each position in city government, there is an office title (director of this, that, or the other thing, policy analyst, or what have you) that an individual puts on a business card. In the background, there is also a civil service title of some kind, which is created by city government and approved by the state's civil service commission. Some require applicants to take a test, and if they score well enough, they earn a position on a list. This is true for a large portion of city positions and will be familiar to those trying to become a police officer or firefighter.

Some civil service titles, however, are exempt from the examination process, but there are few of them, and they are generally reserved for individuals in senior management positions, for political appointees, or for positions requiring highly specialized skills that would be difficult to assess on an exam. There are also citywide titles that do not have a list. These are common to multiple city agencies and are available to any agency for hiring.

We had to identify civil service positions to create the unit, because hiring a candidate directly off the market without using a list was difficult. Thus, we needed an available title that required no exam and that the agency could use. We found one, but it had a major problem—it did not pay a whole heck of a lot. Few matching civil service titles lent themselves well to the type of candidate we hoped to attract. The one available title would allow us to offer only a $38,000 starting salary ($42,700 in 2020 dollars)—a paltry salary to survive on in NYC. Part of the limitation was that data scientists for this type of work were a relatively new phenomenon, and there was not much precedent in the civil service for such employees. There were some titles at the PhD level, but those highly specialized individuals might not want what was otherwise an entry-level position.

Once we had written the job postings with the skillset we sought as well as some of the personality traits crucial in a strong candidate for such a team (think curiosity, for one), we scoured résumés and began the work of finding the best available talent. I worked my network, reaching out to graduate school connections, my professional contacts, and colleagues from multiple city agencies to spread the word that we were looking for a few smart people to form a new unit at the world's largest fire department, which had a massive reservoir of data, including billions of records of emergency-related information going back many years.

ATTRACTING TALENT

Part of the challenge of attracting talent in the public sector is that in many situations, like this one, there are salary limitations. So you instead have to attract people to join your team based on some of the job's intangibles.

Fortunately, in government, I have found that people who want to work in the public sector often share similar foundational values that provide motivation outside of money. Many believe public service is noble. Many want to create change or have an impact on the world. Others want to go to work and feel that they are making a difference. Others, maybe not. Others may want the stability that comes with working in the public sector. Whatever brings them to it, public servants and those attracted to service often have much in common, and teams are formed by attracting people who share common values. The way to attract people with particular values is to live those values as an organization and relentlessly find and promote people who share them.

Team building also matters. Do not underestimate the power of people's need to be part of something bigger than themselves. Little things can help a project identify a team ethos. From a catchy team name to a slogan, mission statement, or even T-shirts, find ways to make members feel that they are part of something special. The FDNY Fire Academy has a giant wall covered with hundreds of patches from every single fire company. Each patch has a special meaning and story that help the company form a unique identity. Yes, they are part of the larger organization, but the patches also show how small teams from across the vast city have unique identities, and you don't have to be a fire company to do something along those lines. Our analytics unit took this to heart by designing their own patch and adding it as a logo to their email signature and to their jobs shirts (the FDNY day-to-day uniform that most members of the department own).

In my case, much of the appeal of my position at the FDNY was the opportunity to be part of a hallowed institution. I remembered watching from my quarters at Fort Sill, Oklahoma (where I was attending the US Army Field Artillery Officer Basic Course in 2001), the images of firefighters and response personnel sifting through the rubble at Ground Zero in lower Manhattan on September 11. Those images were forever emblazoned in my memory. The FDNY lost 343 of its own that day, and it had one of the most critical municipal agency functions—to save lives and protect property. Before working there, I knew that I would be honored to do any job in support of the organization for any period of time.

For this new team we were building, although we could not pay a lot, we could offer the opportunity to work in one of the coolest organizations in the world, with the prospect of doing ride-alongs with fire companies and EMS units, and the chance for our team members to be a firefighter for a day at the FDNY's Fire Academy (an experience that immediately lets you know you should have been a firefighter), learning how to put out car fires, rappel off the side of a high-rise, conduct a rescue beneath a subway car, and carry bunker gear into a burning room.

FINDING A GREAT LEADER

Leaders have incredible impact on the overall team, so for

the team of three analysts and a director, we focused first on finding the director. That way, the person we selected could help build the team and might know candidates who would appreciate the opportunity to work with us, build something new, and be part of an amazing organization. It was likely that a new manager would want to have some say in who the team members would be. However, given how long it would take to hire a new person, I didn't want to wait until the director was fully on board to commence the hiring process for the analyst positions. I had to start that process in conjunction with that for the director position and then do my best to synchronize the two streams of hiring.

We found our director as though by fate. He was working in the organization I had formerly worked for, the Mayor's Office of Operations. I had never met him as we had not overlapped in our employment there, but we had colleagues in common. When I met Jeff Chen, I knew immediately that he would be an amazing fit. Jeff had been overseeing analytical problem solving for the mayor's office and had led a number of fascinating initiatives. Here was an immensely talented professional with a perfect background and a ten-ton brain. I thought he would be ideal to get on board to help build, equip, and train the team, do a few amazing feats of data science, and then (I figured) depart after a short stint with us. Someone like this would be in high demand and would forever keep moving along. We would be lucky to get two years out of him, but in my mind those two years would be invaluable and would set the team up for success.

Although I could not hire him as quickly as I wanted, I did want Jeff to have at least a data scientist or two by the time he started. I coordinated with him after he was selected as our candidate and entered the onboarding process. He identified the top qualities and skills he wanted me to look for in interviewing the analysts—specifically, that they should be curious about how things work and should have some background in data, coding, or statistics. Ideally, the candidates would have worked with R, a computer program used for data analysis and statistical computing, but that was unlikely based on what we were paying. Still, we would look for it.

The team we put together was attracted to the notion that they would be working for someone so talented. Part of my conversations with our top candidates involved presenting the opportunity to come in with curiosity and a fresh perspective, learn as much as they possibly could, conduct operational research projects in an organization with an enduring legacy, and do their part to save lives. The right candidates would see this opportunity as a way to get a foot in the door, learn invaluable skills, and leverage the experience to move into new opportunities down the road—almost like a working graduate program with a stipend. They would also get to be a small part of the organization and have a role in its incredible work. As former Fire Commissioner Sal Cassano used to say, it takes a lot of people to get a truck to the front of a burning building, thus acknowledging all the components that make the organization run—payroll, human resources (HR), budget, fleets, facilities, and so forth. All play a role in saving lives every day.

THE INTERVIEW PROCESS

When attracting new talent, it's important to take time to fully vet the candidates through the interview process. I always rely on interview panels to ensure I have diverse representation from various points within the organization (i.e., reps from teams that might work with the individual, etc.). If you are in a place to support the hiring process, consider creating a candidate rating sheet on which you and the other interview panelists rate candidates on their demonstrated skills, leadership potential, experience, and organizational fit (whether they share the same values). Rating allows you to objectively see how the group perceived an individual, particularly when there are several strong candidates. (See graphic 7.1 for a sample hiring rating sheet.)

Figure 7.1: Sample Hiring Rating Sheet

Rater name: _____

Please rate the candidate in the areas below following the rating scale:
(4) Highly Qualified, (3) Mostly Qualified, (2) Somewhat Qualified, (1) Not Qualified

> Factor Weight can be any level, such as 4, 3, 2, 1, or some high and some low. Give the factors weight according to their relative importance.

CANDIDATE NAME	SHARED VALUES	SKILLSET	EXPERIENCE	LEADERSHIP POTENTIAL	AVERAGE SCORE
Factor Weight	4	3	2	1	Total = 0 to 38
Example: Candidate #1 Sam Jones	4 x 3 = 12	9	8	3	32
Candidate #2					
Candidate #3					
Candidate #4					
Candidate #5					

> Multiply the Factor Weight by the qualification score

> Tally the total score here

Shared Values: The extent to which the candidate aligns with your organization's values

Skillset: The extent to which the candidate can provide expertise in the specific area you are hiring for. List the skills here.

Experience: The extent to which the candidate has performed functions in the type of role or organization for which you are hiring

Leadership Potential: The extent to which the candidate is likely to provide leadership within your organization

In this instance, we put together panel interviews including multiple directors from across the agency who were willing to sit in. Being cognizant of their time, I prepared packets before the interviews with a candidate rating sheet for the interview panel, which included instructions for using the rating sheet, copies of résumés, and a list of sample questions to guide them during the interviews. I was lucky to get busy, important people to support me in this process, including the Chiefs of EMS and Fire Operations who would also be the first clients of the new team.

To further identify good candidates, I invited team members to the panel who were excellent judges of fit to the culture of the organization. They had a sixth sense, or intuition, that was invaluable in the hiring process. In my life, I have been blessed with a number of folks in my professional and personal life who have this skill. Identify those who have it, pay them heed, and hire at your own peril anyone they judge will not be a good fit. One incorrect hire, especially in the public sector (where firing is a long, complicated process), can have a devastating effect on your team. I have heard that in terms of impact, one incorrect hire costs three times the salary the member was paid while on the team.

In this process, we identified our top analyst candidates. Two were top-notch recent college grads who had done substantive data analysis in their coursework and on their senior theses. Both exhibited an intense desire to learn coding but brought novice skills to the table in that area. After speaking with our new director, we agreed that this was the best way to go; he could train the team in developing the needed skills. We began the onboarding process with both of them, and we had an amazing foundation for our new team.

ESTABLISH QUICK WINS

This was my first foray into creating a team with a very specific purpose in city government. From vision to the hiring of our first employee took nine months. Especially because it had taken some time to build the team, once everyone was onboarded, we wanted to establish quick wins.

We had to overcome significant challenges to prove the team's value and integrate it into operations in a way that convinced our main customers (chiefs in operations, fire prevention, and EMS) that it added value. Uniformed services tend to be insular, often skeptical of outsiders who have not shared their experiences. Newcomers sometimes have to prove their mettle before someone in uniform will accept what they have to say, so our new team would have to focus on building relationships early in its tenure. Almost immediately, we sent the new team on ride-alongs with fire operations and EMS. Spending a day with a unit on the ground gave the data team a sense not only of operations and what units did but also of how they did it. When a citizen in NYC calls 911 with a medical emergency or a fire, how does that information go from a 911 call taker to dispatch to a unit arriving on the ground? Once a unit does arrive, how is that data collected? Having a firsthand account of how all of this came together would give the team significant insights into the data itself.

Doing these ride-alongs had another benefit. It helped the team overcome some of the skepticism toward these new, techie, data geeks. Although obviously not the same as serving in uniform, the experience created relationships and gave the team an anchor point from which to discuss data. If you are sitting with a chief to discuss response times and are able to add that when you spent a day with engine company such and such, you can make the chief's ears perk up and make him take the team's data insights a degree or two more seriously. Ride-alongs were time well spent (oh, and they were a lot of fun and a key tool for retention).

The team also needed to generate quick wins to gain favor with key stakeholders in the organization and create value. We did this in a few ways. One strategy was to build inroads with analysts throughout the department who were already doing data analysis. The FDNY at the time comprised over 16,000 people, with dozens doing data analysis for their supervisors and bosses in hundreds of ways. This was terrific! The analytics unit could find those teams, tap into them, and create a training academy to bring them together, discuss leading practices, share with one another, and learn new methods of data analysis from our team. This worked remarkably well, and very quickly, the analytics unit and the various data teams geeked out together on emergency response data.

Our team also looked for ways to save time for the various data analysts throughout the department. By scripting recurring formulas and analysis in a program such as R or Python, the analytics unit could save various data teams significant time and teach them a new skill. One example was in the Office of Recruitment and Diversity (ORD), which had created a mentoring program between firefighters and candidates from the time the latter were called from the civil service list to when they completed the Fire Academy. Pairing these new recruits with experienced firefighters gave the recruits someone to coach and mentor them throughout the hiring process, helping the recruits to complete the Fire Academy. To implement this program, ORD used surveys to collect information about both recruits and potential mentors and matched them based on factors such as ZIP code, favorite sports team, and demographic information. The individual doing the matching spent considerable time using paper to match the mentors and mentees, which was something we knew we could script. Working with ORD, the analytics unit wrote a simple program that allowed the matching to happen rapidly (within seconds) versus the days required for a human to do it on paper. This helped ORD tremendously and gave them a new tool to save their team time and aggravation. This inspired respect between ORD and the analytics unit demonstrated the analytics unit's value when working with other stakeholders.

Once our team was cobbled together, they quickly went to work on complex data questions. They redesigned the risk model for our Risk-Based Inspection System and explored a new frontier in data science—leveraging data to optimize resource allocation. As a result of the team's work, we were able to create Firecast, the fire risk prediction model. The team not only built the mechanics of it but also helped move the fire services forward in exploring new methods for prioritizing the efforts of firefighters in their work to save lives and protect property. The fire services took note, such as in the 2014 *National Fire Protection Association Journal* (Roman 2014), *The Wall Street Journal* (Dwoskin 2014), and *Crain's Business New York* who called it the "Moneyball for firefighting" (McEnery 2014). Clearly, people were interested in learning how data science could help us transform day-to-day municipal operations.

At the end of the day, we found amazing and brilliant people who gave significant time to the team. Our director was there for a year and a half before being accepted by a White House fellowship program. Our other team members stayed longer but eventually found their way to other positions in city government, increasing their pay and data impact.

TIPS FOR MANAGING A TEAM

Once you have a team, focus those individuals, give them direction, and find ways to let them soar. In any leadership role, each decision you make will affect others, will come with risk, and more often than not may seem like choosing between the lesser of two evils. Welcome to management. Ugh.

Despite this, I have found that a couple of key items really keep my top performers on track and those needing to improve focused on key improvements.

ARROW CHARTS

Achieving high performance starts with identifying the most important things and pushing the team to relentlessly pursue those things. At least once a year, my teams conduct a strategic planning exercise, either with a professional facilitator or someone on the team who is skilled at such work. Through this process, the members identify their top three to five key individual contributions for the year, the desired end state (all nested within the team's overall goals), and major milestones along the path from the beginning of the year to the end.

Each member's information is then organized into an arrow chart, a single-page way to display your annual goals with desired end states and major milestones throughout the year to drive your professional performance. To these we tie metrics that we can measure on a regular basis.

I use arrow charts for my personal professional development, and they are equally beneficial for a team. The charts become a great tool for facilitating conversations about barriers to getting things done. (See graphic 7.2 for a sample arrow chart.)

Figure 7.2: Sample Arrow Chart

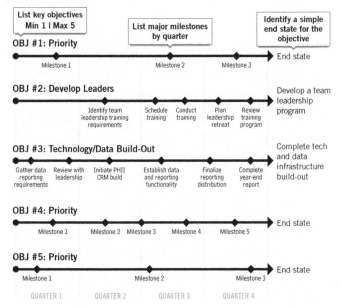

INDIVIDUAL SCORECARDS

After creating an arrow chart, it's helpful to make individual scorecards. Based on individuals' contributions to strategic goals, devise a method for tracking their progress on those goals, their most vital functions, and their overall performance—this is their scorecard.

What gets measured gets managed. This axiom rings true because by taking time to measure something, you bring attention to it. Having your team measure activities related to a key goal automatically brings focus to it, and with focus comes energy.

WEEKLY METRICS HUDDLE

Recurring team meetings to share progress on metrics tied to strategic goals are an absolute must. They maintain focus, energy, and momentum behind the most important goals of the organization, and they let the members of the team hold one another accountable. In my experience, it's most effective to hold such meetings weekly.

GIVE FEEDBACK: THREE UP/THREE DOWN

To support your team in their progress, you must give them regular, consistent, and honest feedback about their performance as team members. Providing feedback consistently and regularly keeps both the employee and the employer on the same page.

In city government, we are officially required to create an annual performance report to meet stipulations in the collective bargaining agreements with unions that represent certain employees. In my mind, however, this is the bare minimum. Feedback must be given on a regular basis to focus a team on what is important and to energize top performers, especially millennials who devour feedback and want to know how they are doing.

There are many ways to do this, and one I find effective is what I call Three Up/Three Down, which I use to give team members an assessment of their strengths and areas for improvement. (See graphic 7.3 for an example of Three Up/Three Down.)

Figure 7.3: Sample Three Up / Three Down

This is a useful tool for providing feedback to employees. I also ask that they complete one to provide me with feedback as their supervisor/manager. This form facilitates discussion of an employee's strengths (to find ways to build on them) and weaknesses (to identify methods for improving and building skills). I always provide three strengths and up to three areas for improvement.

	What you've observed as a supervisor	How you believe they can build on this strength	Steps they can take to build on it
ITEM	**DESCRIPTION**	**PROPOSED**	**POTENTIAL ACTION STEPS**
STRENGTHS			
Example: Strength Item #1 Leading Meetings	You have a strong ability to organize and lead meetings.	Lead more meetings for our team.	Take on organizing and preparing our team's weekly All Hands meeting.
Strength Item #2			
Strength Item #3			
AREAS FOR IMPROVEMENT			
Example: Area for Improvement #1 Business Writing	Your emails are often disorganized and too long, and it is hard to find the main point.	Write shorter, more concise emails that deliver the bottom line up front.	Attend training on business writing, such as ACME Business Writing.
Area for Improvement #2			
Area for Improvement #3			

In this format, I give employees a sense of how they can build on their strengths, and I suggest action steps they should take in their areas for improvement. I provide three of each—that is, three strengths and three areas to improve, or three up and three down. When we follow up the next time around, it is easy to determine whether the employee has taken the action we discussed. If not, this can generate a performance improvement plan or a memorandum for record. If they have taken action and are making improvement, the feedback has fulfilled its purpose.

360° ASSESSMENT

Another tool that I highly recommend for both leaders and their employees is called a 360° assessment, which seeks input from others in the organization to improve personal performance. This is an anonymous survey tool through which the subject receives candid feedback from superiors, peers, and subordinates. The name derived by the intention of giving the subject of the survey a complete view of his/her leadership from all perspectives in an organization.

I have used this tool multiple times throughout my career and learned something about myself and how others perceive my leadership each time. The army requires this of all its leaders at least once every three years as part of its leadership evaluation process. I simply use an online survey tool to share a short survey with both rating questions and short-answer questions for candid feedback.

Note that these should always be anonymous. Don't ask the respondent's name or any identifying information. To determine someone's position in your organization, give position-level responses. Try to keep the categories broad to preserve anonymity. For example, I lumped my boss in with several senior staff respondents.

Consider having people rate you in self-awareness, performance, leadership, teamwork, communication, and in general. For each of those headings, I've asked them to answer three to five questions using the scale Among the Top 10 Percent, Among the Top Third, Typical, Among the Lagging Third, and Among the Lagging 10 Percent. In each section, I provide room for comments.

In the Overall section, I state, "Jeff contributes to my ability to do my job well" and ask the respondents to Strongly Agree, Agree, Neither Agree nor Disagree, Disagree, or Strongly Disagree. Additional items include "Share a specific example of something Jeff does well," "Share an example of something Jeff could improve," and "Are there any other comments you'd like to share with Jeff?"

WORKPLACE CLIMATE SURVEYS

As a leader, you must also seek feedback about the entire organization (or the entire team as applicable) and about how individuals perceive the organization's climate in key areas.

A workplace climate survey is a good tool for understanding how the workplace environment affects your team. When I use workplace climate surveys, I ask how my team feels about the workplace overall, how they feel about their specific team or division, and about equal employment opportunity, followed by general perspectives about the team. Do they enjoy coming to work? Can they give of themselves fully? Do they feel respected, safe, and able to thrive in the workplace? Ask for clarity for any low-rated responses. (See graphic 7.4 for a list of sample questions.)

Figure 7.4:
Sample Workplace Climate Survey Items

What is your work unit/team?

		Strongly Agree	Agree	Neutral	Disagree	Strongly Disagree
1.	I like my job.	O	O	O	O	O
2.	I am able to perform my best at work every day.	O	O	O	O	O
3.	I know what is expected of me at work.	O	O	O	O	O
4.	I have the materials and equipment I need to do my work right.	O	O	O	O	O
5.	At work, I have the opportunity to do what I do best every day.	O	O	O	O	O
6.	In the past seven days, I have received recognition or praise for doing good work.	O	O	O	O	O
7.	My supervisor or someone at work seems to care about me as a person.	O	O	O	O	O
8.	There is someone at work who encourages my development.	O	O	O	O	O
9.	At work, my opinions seem to count.	O	O	O	O	O
10.	The mission/purpose of the organization makes me feel my job is important.	O	O	O	O	O
11.	My associates or coworkers are committed to doing quality work.	O	O	O	O	O
12.	In the past six months, someone at work has talked to me about my progress.	O	O	O	O	O
13.	In the past year, I have had opportunities to learn and grow.	O	O	O	O	O
14.	Most days, I am enthusiastic about my work.	O	O	O	O	O

	Strongly Agree	Agree	Neutral	Disagree	Strongly Disagree
15. I find enjoyment in my work.	O	O	O	O	O
16. I feel mentally worn out.	O	O	O	O	O
17. I feel emotionally worn out.	O	O	O	O	O
18. I think that my skills and other attributes are being utilized.	O	O	O	O	O
19. I am given opportunities to build new skills.	O	O	O	O	O
20. I feel a strong sense of belonging to this organization.	O	O	O	O	O
21. Individuals in my unit/team are encouraged to perform to their fullest potential.	O	O	O	O	O
22. Individuals in my unit/team work well together as a team.	O	O	O	O	O
23. Individuals in my unit/team have access to mentoring opportunities.	O	O	O	O	O
24. Individuals in my unit/team have access to skill development opportunities.	O	O	O	O	O
25. Individuals' skills and other attributes are being put to use.	O	O	O	O	O
26. Individuals' skills and other attributes are taken into account when assigning tasks.	O	O	O	O	O
27. Individuals are recognized for their contributions.	O	O	O	O	O
28. Individuals trust their leadership.	O	O	O	O	O
29. I trust that my unit/team's leadership will support my career advancement.	O	O	O	O	O
30. I trust that my unit/team's leadership will represent my best interests.	O	O	O	O	O

	Strongly Agree	Agree	Neutral	Disagree	Strongly Disagree
31. Leaders in my unit/team are encouraged to perform to their fullest potential.	○	○	○	○	○
32. Leaders in my unit/team are consistent in enforcing policies.	○	○	○	○	○
33. Leaders in my unit/team communicate well with one another.	○	○	○	○	○
34. Leaders in my unit/team communicate well with their team members.	○	○	○	○	○
35. Leaders in my unit/team treat me fairly.	○	○	○	○	○
36. Leaders in my unit/team treat their team members fairly.	○	○	○	○	○
37. Leaders in my unit/team work well together as a team.	○	○	○	○	○
38. Leaders in my unit/team trust their team members.	○	○	○	○	○
39. When high-pressure tasks with short deadlines arise, people in my unit/team do a good job of handling them.	○	○	○	○	○
40. Discipline is administered fairly.	○	○	○	○	○
41. Programs are in place to effectively address individuals' concerns.	○	○	○	○	○
42. Decisions are made after reviewing relevant information.	○	○	○	○	○
43. Relevant job information is shared among personnel.	○	○	○	○	○
44. I feel motivated to give my best efforts to the mission of my unit/team.	○	○	○	○	○
45. Personnel are accountable for their behavior.	○	○	○	○	○
46. My unit/team's performance compared to similar units/teams is high.	○	○	○	○	○

	Strongly Agree	Agree	Neutral	Disagree	Strongly Disagree
47. Efforts are made to make everyone feel like part of the team.	O	O	O	O	O
48. My unit/team makes good use of available resources to accomplish its mission.	O	O	O	O	O
49. I am proud to tell others that I belong to our company/organization.	O	O	O	O	O
50. I feel that I am assigned tasks or projects that are not within my job description.	O	O	O	O	O

Please provide comment. You must provide comment on any responses you rated low.

	Strongly Agree	Agree	Neutral	Disagree	Strongly Disagree
51. All personnel make valuable contributions to the mission of our company/organization.	O	O	O	O	O
52. All personnel are given opportunities to make valuable contributions to the mission of our company/organization.	O	O	O	O	O
53. Qualified personnel of all races/ethnicities can expect similar job assignments.	O	O	O	O	O
54. Qualified personnel of all religions can expect similar job assignments.	O	O	O	O	O
55. Qualified personnel of all genders can expect similar job assignments.	O	O	O	O	O
56. People of all races/ethnicities can expect to be treated with the same level of professionalism.	O	O	O	O	O
57. People of all religions can expect to be treated with the same level of professionalism.	O	O	O	O	O
58. People of all genders can expect to be treated with the same level of professionalism.	O	O	O	O	O

	Strongly Agree	Agree	Neutral	Disagree	Strongly Disagree
59. Qualified personnel of all races/ethnicities can expect the same training opportunities.	O	O	O	O	O
60. Qualified personnel of all religions can expect the same training opportunities.	O	O	O	O	O
61. Qualified personnel of all genders can expect the same training opportunities.	O	O	O	O	O
62. Sexual harassment does not occur in my work area.	O	O	O	O	O
63. Racial slurs are not used in my work area.	O	O	O	O	O
64. Certain people are often reminded of small errors or mistakes they have made in an effort to belittle them.	O	O	O	O	O
65. I have a clear understanding of my role within our company/organization.	O	O	O	O	O
66. I have a clear understanding of my job description.	O	O	O	O	O
67. I have a clear understanding of the standards by which I'm evaluated.	O	O	O	O	O
68. People in my unit/team do *not* practice favoritism.	O	O	O	O	O

If you selected Strongly Disagree or Disagree above, in what way do you perceive favoritism is being displayed?

	Strongly Agree	Agree	Neutral	Disagree	Strongly Disagree
69. To what extent does your leadership promote an office climate based on respect and trust?	O	O	O	O	O

Please provide comments below.

Please note that all comments will be provided to the leadership/management exactly as they are written. Please do not provide any personally identifiable information.

Good times to conduct such surveys include when you are new in a position (to provide a baseline of your team and their perceptions), when some other significant change has occurred, or on a recurring basis, such as annually.

GROWTH OPPORTUNITIES

Professionals want opportunities to learn, grow, and develop in their careers. I have tried everywhere I have worked to put together opportunities and space for employees to grow. I look for ways to invest in individuals who may want to enhance their skills. If those skills are nested within organizational priorities, I find ways to have the organization sponsor the employee's learning. If it is not possible to pay directly for courses, I allow employees to learn during work hours so we can sponsor them with time (again, when that is beneficial to the organization). Giving employees time to do that skill building is a valuable investment.

If your organization lacks the resources to send you or your team to training, find low-cost options online. I have personally taken classes in coding, project management, and other skills online from different companies who provide these services. There are ample ways to develop highly specific skillsets at a low cost.

There are also many opportunities to build skills and grow

at work. If you are the employee, ask for opportunities to sit in on meetings. Offer to take notes or to prep your boss for the meeting, and volunteer to support your boss in building this type of program within your organization. If you lead a team, provide them with opportunities to learn and grow. Create spaces where people can come together to discuss leadership, teamwork, company culture, and more.

Various teams I have worked on have also built centers of excellence and training in which team employees conduct classes for their coworkers, or we've hired consultants to provide training. I have also built leadership development opportunities for those who want them, following a model of coaching and mentoring individuals two levels down. This gives employees at various levels of the organization the ability to connect with senior leadership in ways they may not otherwise have access to, and it allows senior leadership to inculcate the organization's values at a different level. In these meetings, I have found that most, but not all, employees are eager to be part of and contribute to the exercises and discussions. That is indicative of who is interested in growing in the organization and willing to put in a small amount of effort to do so.

To put together such a program requires effort but not a significant amount. I have put together my own professional development agenda, and I've also had employees do so. I use the first session of these to allow the team to identify what it wants to learn and how. Sessions can be as simple as reading a short article or other text ahead of time and coming together to discuss it. Leadership, time management, handling workplace conflict, and social styles are all topics that employees on my various teams have asked to discuss. The bottom line is finding ways to train the team that are low cost and don't require a significant amount of time or other resources.

Building and leading teams in the confines of government is no easy feat and requires people dedicated to pushing and pursuing these programs. Those who take the time to invest in building and focusing their team, championing their people, listening and engaging with them, and investing in their development will find that it results in greater engagement and productivity from their staff. I think of the best people I have worked for. They all believed in me, gave me opportunities to grow, learn, and experience new things, and pushed me to be better. Winning organizations invest in their people and make training part of what they do.

KEY TAKEAWAYS

Building a team is the most important work you may ever have to do. It is critical to attract and retain the best people who share your organization's values. In the public sector, this can be challenging because we cannot always compete on salary with the private sector. However, we can offer meaningful work, an opportunity to be part of something bigger than oneself, and chances to experience things others never will. Take the time to build a team with the right people. One wrong move can be very costly to an organization and wreak havoc, particularly in the public sector where hiring and firing can be very slow processes.

When you find the right people, though, invest in them. Provide opportunities for them to grow professionally and to learn new skills. There are many low-cost ways to do this today. Create forums to provide feedback to your employees on ways they can improve and how they can build on their strengths. Give them measurable goals and check in on their progress regularly. Knowing what is expected of them and seeing their progress not only helps a team member focus but also provides a sense of accomplishment (or reveals where changes are necessary). Finally, create a way to measure the climate of the workplace, the team, and leadership to make sure you are creating the type of environment you envision.

The tools in this chapter will help you build world-class teams that accomplish amazing things. Even in a challenging system with no cash rewards or stock incentives, with the right team, you can get things done nonetheless.

CHAPTER 8

GOVERNMENT STARTUP

Putting principles of action to work to build something new in a bureaucratic organization takes patience, persistence, and a plan. Here is a look at how we did it in NYC government, building the first new city agency in over twenty years.

"Resistance to change is proportional to how much the future might be altered by any given act."

—STEPHEN KING

In my office at the TLC, where I was the Deputy Commissioner of Policy and External Affairs, I leaned over my daily planning sheet at my desk preparing for the day. It was early morning, before most people had arrived for the workday. I spotted a notification on my phone for an article that caught my eye: "NYC to Launch New Department of Veterans' Services to Help City Vets Find Housing, Jobs, and Medical Care" (Durkin 2015). It explained that NYC was creating a new city agency, the NYC Department of Veterans' Services, to provide support and services to military veterans and service members, the first municipal agency of its kind in the United States. The law would take effect in April 2016, and the existing Mayor's Office of Veterans' Affairs, a four-person team mostly involved in ceremonial duties for the NYC veterans' community, would morph into the new city agency.

This was very exciting to me. As a city employee with nearly a decade of city government experience and over fifteen years of military experience who still served as an active member in the Army National Guard, I thought this was a fascinating project to which I could lend support. I knew nothing of the people who were launching this organization, neither the leadership nor those mentioned in the news article, but I did some digging. A former colleague at the FDNY was tied to the current mayoral administration, so I reached out to ask her whether there was a point person for establishing the agency. Within a day or two, I heard back from the Commissioner of the Mayor's Office of Veterans' Affairs, who would oversee the transition of this small office into a full-fledged city agency. Her assistant said that the commissioner wanted to have coffee with me, so we set the details.

I didn't know it yet at the time, but I was about to start one of my most challenging and rewarding projects.

AN UNCOMMON LEADER AND AN INSPIRING ORGANIZATION

I did my research on General Sutton and found out a little about her prior to our coffee. She had retired after thirty-five years of military service as a brigadier general and an army doctor. Also, we had both served at different times in the Multinational Force and Observers, the army's small contingent of soldiers who helped maintain the 1979 peace treaty between Egypt and Israel. I liked her background and thought that I might be able to help her and the city in some small way.

I arrived early at the coffee shop a block over from city hall and secured a table to make sure we could quickly connect and get down to business when she arrived. The moment she entered the coffee shop, the place transformed. She brought energy, passion, and enthusiasm with her very being. The whole room felt it and lit up when she walked in.

She walked toward the table, somehow sensing that I was the guy awaiting her arrival. Thrusting her hand out with a big smile, she said, "Hello, you must be Jeffrey. I'm Loree Sutton." She sat down across from me and hoisted a silver, latch-style briefcase to the top of the table. From within, she pulled out her vision for the Department of Veterans' Services (DVS) and laid it in front of me. She jumped right into an impassioned explanation of how the new agency would focus on supporting veterans, from those who needed a lot of support (chronically homeless veterans) to those who wanted to build a business, get a degree, or start a family. She wanted every veteran of military service to know that NYC was the place to do those very things after separating from the military.

After her time in the army, General Sutton had been named commissioner of the NYC Mayor's Office of Veterans' Affairs. She came with several big ideas on how to address the cost and social stigma of mental healthcare that so often affects veterans. Her model included multiple pathways and modalities of care that could provide much-needed support to veterans struggling with mental illness or the trauma of war. It offered a means for finding support outside clinical services—the care with the highest cost and social stigma.

The transition from a small office of four employees to a team of thirty-six was already underway, and she was looking to put together her senior leadership team. She explained to me that the team would be a flat matrix organization with lots of dotted lines among various team members supporting one another's projects and programs. There would be three lines of action (LOAs) or units within the organization, each focused on different areas of support for veterans. One would focus on housing, specifically on supporting homeless veterans. A second would connect veterans to a host of mental health resources, steering away from a purely clinical approach to all veterans' issues and instead building out a range of support from cultural events and peer connections to mentoring programs, holistic services, and of course clinical help when necessary. The third LOA would focus on supporting veterans who needed help in finding jobs, starting a company, or getting an education. Her emphasis was on peer-to-peer models or having veterans (or those tied to the veterans' community) work in each of these LOAs to help NYC veterans connect and find services.

She spelled it out passionately as we sipped our coffee and took in the vision. Having built teams in city government in the past, I knew that building a team of thirty-six from a team of four would be no easy feat. I also knew that the hurdles to creating change in government would be monumental not because of a lack of vision, strategy, or leadership, but because the oomph necessary to accomplish tasks in an environment not designed for change demands Herculean strength. I often thought of Stephen King's *11/22/63*, in which the protagonist discovers a wormhole to travel back in time to try to prevent the assassination of President John F. Kennedy. He finds that history doesn't want to change and that it will throw hurdles in his path at every turn to prevent any influence that might alter its course. Bureaucracies don't want to change and will erect every imaginable roadblock to hold you back. The key ingredients to overcoming its obstacles are grit, determination, and persistence.

I knew in that moment at the coffee shop that I was hooked. This was an uncommon leader, and I couldn't help thinking how lucky NYC was to have someone like General Sutton at the helm when launching a new agency. I wanted to work with her, be in her orbit, and part of whatever she was doing. Shortly after that initial conversation, I joined Commissioner Sutton as her deputy commissioner to shoulder the awesome responsibility of stewarding this new organization into existence. I was completely taken by her belief in how much good could be done if we got this right. On the one hand, I was deeply humbled when she asked me to join her. On the other hand, I knew to buckle up. This was going to be quite the ride.

A BUREAUCRATIC STARTUP WITH PLENTY OF CHALLENGES

What I found when I first joined DVS, six months after the initial coffee with General Sutton, was that this was truly a startup in every sense of the word. We had received some funding from the city's coffers to establish the agency, but we had little to no equipment, no ability to purchase anything, no computers or phones, not a single manual, guide, or handbook to help us operate. And we did not yet have people in place to do the work. Although we were a fledgling city government agency, we faced the same struggles as any other startup with one very significant difference: we had to build this thing in the context of city bureaucracy.

We were building a new organization within the behemoth framework of NYC government, something that had not been tried for nearly twenty years. The last agency to pop up was in the late 1990s when the city had created the Office of Emergency Management. Although there is an abundance of life and death of city organizations—a unit added here, a merger there, leadership changes, and reorganization of functions within and across city agencies—establishing an agency with a whole new set of functions was uncommon, and we found that navigating this path brought a number of challenges.

After I started, I received the agency's blueprint from a task force that had convened prior to my joining. They had made a plan for funding the agency and building out the structure. As the work of building this organization got underway and we grew the team, we quickly realized that the initial design of the organization required more depth. We had senior leader roles in the agency but no teams supporting them. For example, our chief information officer (CIO) was a team of one person—the CIO. We had to find a way to increase our budget and headcount to grow the size of the teams at a time when the city was facing a severely constrained budget. The city of New York was under a hiring freeze, making it very difficult to obtain the necessary approvals. We were also not excused (or immune) to the city's freezing and thawing of hiring (due to budget constraints). As a result, we often had to do without key vacancies (such as our CIO role that went vacant for over a year before we were approved to rehire).

We also had to build our data systems and recordkeeping processes. We had no official database of record for our clients, and we desperately needed a client relationship manager (CRM) to track our clients and their information. As the team grew, we quickly outgrew our office space and at a pace much faster than we could identify and procure new space. People hunkered down in conference rooms and in any nook or cranny they could find to set about doing the important work of our agency. These were just a few of the many and varied tests that presented themselves to us every day.

The challenges were plenty, and few people in government were familiar with the concept of a startup. At every turn, there was limited understanding of what we were up against, and there was certainly little to no experience with it. For this little agency that could, that needed to establish itself quickly, time was urgent. It all came down to a very simple reality—the city's processes for hiring, procurement, and getting things done operated at a snail's pace. Things were disjointed and required flexible, nimble leadership and employees to cover and fill in the gaps. We had to build the plane while flying it. The pressure from our stakeholders was to deliver results and fast.

FOCUS ON THE MOST PRESSING TARGET

The tension between the pace a startup requires and the context of city government led me to view organizational problems in a different way. Historically, I viewed problems deliberately by dissecting them, identifying next steps, and pursuing each component piece. In this case, however, for each significant challenge we faced, I had to break it down to the immediate next steps, and when there were multiple steps and limited resources, I had to identify the most pressing target first. I focused energy and attention on knocking that target down, while disregarding all else. That is, we distilled every obstacle with multiple urgent and critical components into those that were of highest risk to our existence as a fledgling organization. We would focus our aim there, knock it down, then move on to the next target. The targets came too fast and required too quick a response to give them more attention than what was necessary to take immediate action and move on to the next problem from there.

An example was how we handled the administrative functions of the agency. Like any city agency, we required a number of administrative functions to support our back-office operations, including general human resources (HR) support, budget, fiscal, procurement, payroll, and timekeeping. Yet we had no funding for administrative personnel. Initially, we received administrative support from a sister city agency. They could not support us long term, though, and their support was set to expire before we had fully onboarded the permanent personnel who would do this work in our agency. This presented us with a mammoth problem with no easy solution. Essentially, the operational and administrative functions of our agency were to be performed by our sister agency, but that same agency said it would support us for only another couple of months. The city would not fund us for additional personnel to bring in the right professionals to oversee these functions internally. What could we do?

We recognized that not having these administrative functions would be dire. It was all hands on deck to address this pressing target. We decided to find top performers in our agency who could take on these functions temporarily while doing their current jobs, and then train our new hires in the functions once they were hired. We identified three personnel whom we could train quickly to conduct payroll and timekeeping, HR, and fiscal. They shadowed employees at our sister agency to learn the requisite skills and then performed the functions while we resubmitted our request for new employees, which we could do only every six months. Having these employees do this administrative work in the short term meant pulling them away from the programmatic work that they were already doing, but it also meant that we could limp along until the next funding cycle.

KEEP AN EYE ON FUTURE TARGETS

Even though the immediate targets came at us fast and furiously, we had to keep an eye on the future targets as well. We conducted regular strategic planning sessions as a team to identify the most critical elements that the organization needed but that weren't immediately urgent. If we didn't focus attention and energy on future targets, we knew that they would someday hit us hard. It was far better to reckon with them sooner when they were still only ankle biters.

For example, city employees are hired into civil service titles in government. The city and its agencies have hundreds, if not thousands, of titles, and each specifies the role, salary, and responsibilities of an employee serving under that title. Early in our life as an agency, we were borrowing civil service titles from our sister agency and using citywide available titles. Eventually, our sister agency would need those titles back, and relying solely on citywide available titles limited our ability to tailor the job specifications to precisely what we needed. Additionally, many of these titles are represented by labor unions that have contracts with the city. This includes agreements and restrictions on some of the titles, which may or may not have worked for our unique organizational business model. Establishing a priority to get this work done was critical, but it often competed with the more urgent tasks, such as paying the bills and keeping the lights on. However, not focusing any time and attention on that dilemma was also not an option.

We established a working group that met regularly to lead us through the process of creating these titles, which required both city and state government action. It was a long process. It required diligence to keep it moving forward, one inch at a time, toward a place where the agency had the titles it needed to hire the people to do the work of serving veterans. Even though it never moved as quickly as I would have liked, it moved along as best it could. Even a little time, effort, and energy dedicated to this important work meant that when the time did come for it to be urgent, we were already well along the path to its completion.

SYNCHRONIZE EFFORTS

Those early days were chaotic, as employees wore multiple hats and served in multiple roles. Ensuring that we all stayed on the same page, if that was even possible, required consistent synchronization of actions across the organization. Get this right, and there will simply be no stopping what you can do. By identifying what needs to happen (and when) and aligning resources behind those actions, even mediocre organizations will produce achievement because when aimed in the right direction, the tiny actions of individuals will combine and result in massive action.

I've often used a synchronization matrix that allows me to shape and track the efforts of multiple teams that are conducting simultaneous efforts. In this, I look at the significant activities, key events, and milestones of each team or unit. The format I usually follow looks like a timeline, broken down by unit or team or by project and it displays those efforts across time. This will give you a visual of where efforts are aligned or misaligned within an organization.

HIRING IS CRITICAL

I also learned the need to take time when deciding who to hire to join the team, particularly important in a startup. Early in our startup days, partially out of a need to get people onboarded and partially because we lacked a robust hiring process, we moved quickly to onboard candidates we liked. A couple of our initial key hires were not the right fit for the organization.

Previous to this role, I had served in larger, well-established organizations. Although a poor hiring decision could still have an impact, these organizations could better absorb those impacts along with the secondary and tertiary effects to the culture and well-being of the team by hiring someone whose values do not align with the organization. In a startup where each member is so very critical to the team, you must get each hire right. For one senior position in particular, we hired a candidate that our agency staff did not feel was a good fit but had the background we needed. We proceeded with the hiring anyway. From my perspective, the individual turned out to be a disruptor to the work we were trying to do, had a leadership style that was counter to the culture we were trying to build, and ultimately left after doing significant damage to our fledgling team.

Apart from a few hard lessons I learned, overall I am immensely proud of the people we hired. We did build a team of highly dedicated professionals who shared our values and were committed to building this agency into a leading example of serving veterans and service members. Our team, at the time of the writing of this book, was majority minority, had LGBT representation, and was two-thirds veteran. Or actually 100 percent veteran because, as my boss used to say, we hired only veterans—veterans of service. Everyone on the team had a background of service in some form or fashion to country, community, or cause. It was by hiring these dedicated people that our agency was able to overcome the myriad of challenges we faced and better service our city's military veterans and service members.

LISTEN TO EXPERTS, BUT TRUST YOUR INSTINCTS

Startup life isn't for everyone. It's a life full of hard things that aren't always so easily navigated. "That's the hard thing about hard things—there is no formula for dealing with them," Ben Horowitz (2014) reminds us in his book *The Hard Thing about Hard Things: Building a Business When There Are No Easy Answers.* His was one of the books that reminded me that others were fighting similar battles to ours and encouraged me to keep going. There was no playbook for what we were doing. There was no agency toolkit that laid out how to turn on all the functions in a precise method to get from point A to point B and so on, nothing that told us what to do at each step along the way.

It was in these times where it was important to listen to the experts. We needed them to help us build this organization from the ground up. Not anyone of us on the team could fully be an expert in all things related to building and running a city agency. Although we all had different experiences and backgrounds that allowed us to tackle these issues head-on, we also knew we needed to hear from others to make sure we had all the information we required. We pulled in experts whenever possible to help us frame our challenges and decide on the best routes forward.

Early in our life as a city agency, we pulled in a consulting team that helped us define the basic operating model for the agency. This helped us identify and think through the main areas where we needed to focus effort and energy to build out our functions. They identified all of the critical components of a city agency and highlighted where we were in building capacity in each. It was a very healthy exercise. It gave us a path for moving the agency forward, well scrutinized by experts who validated the model, and it was an immense help to us as we steered the ship.

Although it is important to get the experts to help identify areas where more can be done, it is also important to listen to your own instincts. Even a perfectly vetted project plan or roadmap can be invaluable in helping you navigate the trickiness of organizational leadership, but also listen to that still, small inner voice that nags you about some problem or issue. That isn't to say that these things are in tension; they probably aren't. I learned, however, that even though I often spent considerable time involving others for their perspective and opinions about our challenges, no one knew them better than we did. The issue or task list that keeps coming back and flicking you in the ear, day after day, must be reckoned with. Listen to that and get to work on it!

MAKE TIME FOR YOURSELF

I also found through the experience that self-care is not just a buzzword but an absolute must. As a public servant, especially in an environment that is intense, fast paced, and unforgiving, one needs to create ways to step back, recharge, and find the inner strength to return with a fresh commitment. Too many times, I did not do those things, putting the mission before my own well-being, which often caught up with me in the form of mental and physical burnout. That is never good, and building something with intense attention, care, and energy requires recharging to endure the marathon. Being crammed in a small space with limited ability to think, I often found myself sitting outside on a park bench to read or review reports that needed my attention. Something as simple as that got me outside in the fresh air and away from unceasing distractions.

Self-care is an important component of personal management. In this role, I had to find ways to add more value, focusing on the most important things in the optimal amounts. To do this, I used a number of personal tools that helped me focus my energy and time in the right places. At the beginning of each week, I created a weekly schedule. No, not printing my Outlook calendar for the week and knowing when I have meetings scheduled. Rather, I reviewed my calendar to ensure that what was scheduled supported my goals. If something did not, I canceled it or rescheduled it. I learned to say no to a lot of things. I also found blocks of time to work on my key focus areas. When my calendar was filled during a week for recurring meetings that I did not want to reschedule, I scheduled time between them for my priority tasks for the week. I also used early mornings or evenings, when distractions were minimal, to address key items. Sometimes you may have to get up early and focus on a task a few times per week. I recommend that everyone try one day a week as an early day to get up and work on a very important goal. In no time, you'll find that your productivity accelerates, and you may very well convert other days to early days as well.

KEY TAKEAWAYS

Startups present unique challenges. Building something from the ground up and anticipating all the challenges that will come as you do it is intensely hard work and also intensely gratifying. Being able to say you were the first at something, to navigate tricky waters, to be okay when things don't go according to plan, and to endure the onslaught of obstacles that come your way on a daily basis is no easy feat. But you get to leave your mark and create something new. That is the tradeoff.

In this environment, it is important to keep your focus on the most immediate targets first—those that are taking aim at you and are urgent and critical. As you knock those down, scan the horizon for those distant targets that may be approaching your position and get after them, too.

Your team is your most precious entity. When building a team, if you get this wrong, you will pay the exponential cost of poor decision making. Get this right and there is no stopping you.

Ask for help all along the way. You cannot be an expert in all things at all times. Ask others for their guidance and to do some of the thinking you won't have time for. They can take a lot off your plate. That said, never place anything in front of your instincts. Trust what you hear internally.

Self-care can't just be a buzzword you toss about in this type of environment. You have to do it and allow others on your team to do it, too. Stepping away for a little bit of respite is often when the ideas and inspiration will start to flow once again.

CHAPTER 9

KNOCKOUT

There will be times when you or your project is criticized. It happens to all people, projects, or programs that try to create change. Here are some lessons on how to endure the heat.

"Do not judge me by my successes; judge me by how many times I fell down and got back up again."

—NELSON MANDELA

The local papers were very excited about this city council hearing. The medallion system in NYC was nearing collapse as ride-hailing apps such as Uber and Lyft waged war on the legacy taxicab industry in municipalities across the globe. NYC was hard hit as some taxi drivers, who had invested in taxi medallions that allowed the owner to operate a taxicab in the city, struggled to earn enough fare revenue to meet their financial obligations for massive loans, some in excess of a million dollars for the one-time lucrative business and promise of the American dream. Lured into owning a piece of the taxicab business, many in the industry faced financial catastrophe, some even to the point of deep depression and suicide as *The New York Times* had reported in October 2018 (Fitzsimmons 2018).

The mayor and city council had recently gone back and forth on how to solve the problem. The city council called for a bailout of the industry, arguing that the city was complicit in the crisis because it had auctioned medallions and made millions from their sales. The mayor, meanwhile, was on record as saying that that was simply not a fiscally feasible option (Rosenthal 2019a). Sadly, many of those suffering were immigrants whose dreams of financial independence evaporated as would-be taxi riders turned to app-based companies and demand for taxi rides plummeted.

Here I sat, confronted by cameras at a large table before the NYC Council Committee on Rules, Elections, and Privileges. With microphones arranged in a horseshoe in front of me, I faced the panel of council members watching me behind their large tables in a committee room just off the flank of the city council chambers at city hall. This was my confirmation hearing for Chair and Commissioner of the NYC TLC, where I had worked three years earlier, and I was about to be torn apart. I just didn't know it yet.

It would be one of the most difficult, humbling experiences of my career, but it would teach me many valuable lessons.

ONE DOOR CLOSES, ANOTHER OPENS

Eight weeks prior to this, I had received a text message from a key member of the mayor's team, who asked if I had time for a quick chat that morning. I had sent her my résumé a few months earlier so she could keep me in mind for any positions that might come along.

And one had.

Looking at my background in military operations and city management, she thought I would be a strong candidate for the city's emergency management chief. Almost immediately, I was scheduled for interviews at city hall with the staffs of two key deputy mayors. I interviewed with them and listened to the team's explanation of the key priorities. At the core of that discussion was a need for someone to transform the agency's technology. Yes, please! Right in my wheelhouse.

From there, I was invited to additional interviews with key city hall leadership. I also met with a leading academic who advised the mayor on emergency management policy and wanted to assess my knowledge of the subject. I traveled one morning to his office at Columbia University in upper Manhattan, where he was on the faculty, and sat across from his desk in a small, windowless office. He was passionate about the topic, and we really hit it off. We had a natural chemistry, and our conversation about the city and its role in both preventing and managing risk energized me.

I felt that those conversations went very well, and I was eager for the next step, which was to interview with the mayor.

The call to interview with the mayor never came.

I stood in the wings for a couple of weeks, feeling down about having lost the opportunity but also affirmed for being considered for such a high position, and my connections to people in city hall had expanded in the process, which was a very enjoyable, positive experience.

Then a call came. I was told frankly that although I was a strong candidate, another had been found who had extensive experience with the Federal Emergency Management Agency. Her background sounded exactly right for that role. I expressed my appreciation for the opportunity to be considered.

"There is something else we want to explore with you," said the director of the Mayor's Office of Appointments.

Her job and that of her team was to find people for key appointments in the administration. "We want to consider you for the Taxi and Limousine Commission."

I paused for a moment. I had worked there in the past for a year and a half. It was an interesting tour of duty, as I like to call it. The TLC regulated industries that were currently in the midst of unprecedented change. Leading those industries and their various and competing stakeholders would be no easy feat, but having an opportunity to shape policy on such a large scale met my desire to make a difference. It was something that spoke to my urban planning background. I wanted to try for it! I would have to interview with city hall people for this position, and they made all that happen very quickly. I was then told that I would receive a call from the mayor's assistant to schedule a time for me to interview with the big guy himself.

How cool!

I was called early that same evening and asked whether I could meet the mayor in the evening the next day. "Of course I can," I said. I mean, why would I not be flexible for that? I would travel to Gracie Mansion, the official residence of the mayor of New York on the Upper East Side. "Done!" I was very excited. I had worked very hard for twelve years for an opportunity like this. Even if nothing came of it, a chance to meet with the mayor for even a few minutes to share my thoughts on leading a city agency would be an incredible experience.

THE FIRST HURDLE: SECURING THE NOMINATION

The first hurdle in any political appointment is securing the nomination. In my case, that meant winning over the mayor.

I called a few colleagues who knew the mayor well and could give me some insight into how best to prepare. A contact who had debriefed me on my interviews at city hall for the emergency management position mentioned that although everyone really liked me and my background, I was a little too nice. They thought I should talk about how I could command a situation. With over twenty years of experience successfully leading teams of various sizes in the military, I knew how to take charge of a situation. I simply needed to demonstrate this strength and ability to command to the mayor. I had a specific set of policy and organizational tasks that I would implement immediately if I was appointed to the role. I wanted him to understand that.

I headed to Gracie Mansion from my apartment in Brooklyn with plenty of time to spare. I planned for the subway commute to take at least an hour and added buffer time to be in the area well in advance of the meeting. I got to a nearby park a little early and sat on a bench. I reviewed my notes. I took a moment to meditate. As a young man, I had moved to NYC knowing no one except two or three classmates who moved here after grad school. Now, here I was, sitting outside Gracie Mansion, about to meet the mayor for a job interview. I felt the summer breeze off the East River and breathed deeply. Life was amazing.

I entered the security gate to Gracie Mansion and was met by a police officer who seemed to be expecting me.

"Mr. Roth?" he asked, leading me to a side entrance to the mansion. An aide greeted me there and showed me into the Peach Room. A few minutes later, a lovely young woman entered and let me know that the mayor would be in within a few minutes and that I should make myself comfortable. There was coffee and water on a small table and food on the coffee table. I didn't want to be sitting when the mayor walked in, and I didn't know which seat to take. There was a couch, two chairs opposite it, a fire-place, and beautiful artwork on the walls on loan from a museum.

When he entered the room, all six feet, six inches of him, I did not expect that we'd spend over an hour discussing all things related to the taxi and for-hire vehicle indus-try in NYC. I wasn't expecting five minutes with the guy, but here we were. He invited me to sit in a chair next to him. He slumped into a chair with a folder that had my résumé and some other materials in it. He dived right into the discussion and started by addressing the one concern directly with me.

"You are a nice guy, but that shouldn't be mistaken for weakness," he said, and I felt affirmed. We also discussed how to weather the storm of political attacks that would inevitably follow this role if I was appointed. Little did I know how true this would be as I walked out the gate of Gracie Mansion after that interview. We ended the conversation with a handshake, and he said I would be hearing something very soon.

I received a call a few days later saying that I needed to be vetted by the Mayor's Office of Appointments. For three hours, they asked very detailed questions about all my business dealings, interest in taxicab medallions, and the history of my social media. I'm a pretty simple guy who keeps to himself, so there was not much to report.

Another couple of days went by, and I was called by the deputy mayor who oversaw the TLC. She offered me the job. I was very excited, and I immediately accepted.

LESSON #1: REHEARSE *EVERYTHING*

Now the hard part began. I would appear before the city

council a month later to be confirmed by the council's Committee on Rules, Elections, and Privileges. For this role, the city council advises the mayor and consents to the nominee, one of only two positions that require this process; all other commissioner positions are simply appointed by the mayor with no confirmation by the council. To prepare, I would meet with key city council leadership, including the speaker of the city council.

There are several things I would change if I could redo this entire experience, but one of the key things I got right was the importance of preparation. I was not taking anything for granted. I had not worked in this world for over three years, and even though it personally interested me, I had not followed every news story, rule changes, or issues that had come out of the industry during those years. I was fully engaged in veterans' issues and building a brand-new city agency. To make up for this, I poured myself into preparation. I rehearsed the heck out of this confirmation hearing, and it was necessary. Had I not rehearsed as many times as I did with help from others, it could have gone much worse.

To get the most out of your rehearsals, they should simulate the true conditions as much as possible. If anything, your rehearsals should be more challenging than the real situation so that you are prepared not only for the questions you might face in the hearing but also the stress you will feel. In my case, I had diverse audiences grill me with questions multiple times leading up to the hearing date.

A team at city hall comprising the Mayor's Office of Appointments, the city legislative affairs team (which manages the complex interplay between city hall and the city council), the law department, the mayor's counsel, and the deputy mayor's team all scheduled multiple preparatory sessions to help me frame my answers to questions. They explained that the council would ask questions to force me to make public commitments or discuss the details of legislation, all of which was not ideal in the setting of a public hearing that would be livestreamed, recorded, and transcribed. We had to demonstrate that I had a plan for tackling the problems facing the TLC and its regulated industries but not get bogged down in details that could damage me or the agency.

The preparation was not easy. I sat on one side of a vast conference room table at an office building across from city hall while twenty people sat on the other side and fired question after question at me. These were questions that the team thought the city council would ask and those that I would need to answer in a way that avoided the conflicts just mentioned. All this was coming at a time when the mayor and the city council speaker had different policy views, and the two of them were often at loggerheads.

What made this hearing even more challenging was the fact that the speaker was considering a run for mayor, and the mayor was running for president. Yes, of the United States.

The hearing was scheduled for a Thursday, the day I was supposed to report to my National Guard unit for my obligatory annual two weeks of training. This was something scheduled the year prior that had been mentioned to both the mayor's team and the city council.

The timing was not ideal, but my National Guard unit was extremely supportive and allowed me to report late to training (although I would make up the days at a future training). They would also work with me if I needed to leave training to return to the city for any other hearings related to the position. This moment reminded me how those with whom I have served in uniform have always had my back.

LESSON #2: PLAY TO YOUR STRENGTHS

We all have different strengths, and success is often determined by how well we can leverage those strengths. Especially in a situation like political appointment, in which you are examined under a highly critical microscope, you need to know your strengths and use them as a method of attack.

Personally, I never look forward to hearings. My strength lies in smaller group meetings where I can get to know a person and really engage. Because I am good at one-on-one relationship building, I should have proactively leveraged that strength to meet with as many members of the committee as possible. It should have been a key part of my playbook, which would have shaped the confirmation hearing. Especially because hearings are not my strength, I needed to be able to build relationships with the city council.

Unfortunately, it was a busy summer for city hall. Even though my instinct was to reach out and spend time meeting with council members to introduce myself and some of my ideas for the TLC, we focused only on a couple of cursory meetings that did not go into the depth that I would have liked. Two key meetings in particular did not go how I wished.

The first of those meetings was during the week leading up to the hearing with the city council's chair of the transportation committee, with whom I had worked off and on during my previous stint at the TLC. I had a lot of respect for him and his thoughtfulness on taxi industry issues. Even though he didn't always agree with me or my boss, he was a good partner. We had regularly checked in with him, and I appreciated his willingness to engage in discussion about issues and potential policies. He was also an immigrant and a public servant who seemed deeply committed to his constituency, and I respected that.

When we met, his chief of staff was seated with him, and with me was a member of the mayor's city legislative affairs team. I felt that the meeting started off somewhat strained as the council member was upset about having very little time to review a recent press release from city hall, something completely unrelated to me or my confirmation process. The mayor's office rep listened and then redirected the conversation, which was focused and direct but not tense. It was about what I had expected from this meeting. We discussed in some detail the council member's main concerns and the hot issues in the taxi industries in NYC. It was a productive conversation, and it was clear that we would be able to work together.

Following this conversation, I had a meeting with the speaker of the city council the day prior to the confirmation hearing. A member of the speaker's staff joined me and a rep from the mayor's office. Just before walking to the meeting at city hall, I was told that I should expect the speaker to be amiable and that he would likely try to get to know me and a bit about my personal life.

That was not how the meeting went. The speaker shook my hand, sat down across a table from me, and handed the conversation off to his chief of staff, who did most of the talking. The speaker seemed to me to be distracted by his phone and didn't ask me questions, but his chief of staff gave me insights into questions that the council might ask at the hearing. Both the mayor's rep and I tried to bring some detail to the conversation, but it was a non-starter. What I felt was an icy reception that seemed to make clear to me that the speaker was not interested in knowing me, hearing any of my ideas, or establishing any sort of working relationship.

I sensed that he was gearing up to attack me.

THE MOMENT OF TRUTH: THE HEARING

The morning of the hearing, I met early with the city hall team, which joined me as I walked to city hall's council chambers. As we entered city hall, a place that has always taken my breath away, I grew nervous, mainly because the media would pay attention to this hearing. I had testified on a couple of occasions in the past but never solo and never when I sensed that the political stakes were this high. In the days leading up to this, I had rehearsed, practiced, and researched all the issues as best I could. It was not enough, however.

I set my notes on the table where, in a few minutes, I would give my testimony and answer questions from city council members for as long as they had questions. I had prepared an opening statement focused on who I was and how my experiences shaped the leader I always strove to be. I would also disclose, albeit at a very high level, how I would approach any number of challenges that the TLC faced. The general idea was not to get into specifics but present the picture that I was going to the TLC to dive into these issues. It was on the specifics that they could corner me into speaking out and committing to some policy action or view that might be counter to something the mayor had said publicly. I had to balance that tactic with what the speaker's chief of staff had told me the day before: that they would get specific. I found the situation difficult. I could not brazenly counter anything the mayor had said, yet I had to be specific enough to demonstrate command of the subject matter and discuss how I would approach problems. Oh, and also try to showcase my authentic self.

In the end, I didn't do any of them well.

LESSON #3: SLOW THINGS DOWN

The hearing started with opening remarks by the chair of the committee, who had me sworn in and then asked if I would like to offer any opening remarks, which I did. I read my statement. As soon as I had finished, the speaker of the city council, who had joined the hearing, asked for permission to lead off the questioning. The chair granted it.

That's when it started.

I thought he came in hot and loud. It seemed like he wanted to communicate that this was his turf, and he was going to make everyone, me especially, know that he was in charge of these issues.

The questions came at a rapid pace. Even with all my preparation, the pace was grueling and stressful, compounded by the many cameras and lights trained on me.

The faster the pace, the more pressure and the more likely you are to make a mistake or not answer a question as well as you could. To perform your best, you need to slow things down. The pace was set by those asking the questions, but I could have slowed the tempo by taking a little time to gather my thoughts before jumping in with a response. Maybe sip water or scrawl a note before replying, anything to buy a little time to answer questions.

LESSON #4: BE AUTHENTIC

Despite the rapid pace, I tried to hold my own by being responsive, saying enough to address the question and keep moving. The problem was, it seemed to me that the speaker of the city council wanted me to commit to things I could not commit to.

"Do you think that the TLC should apologize to the medallion owners who have suffered so greatly because of the... overly inflated value of those medallions? Would you apologize if you were commissioner and chair of the TLC? Would you do that today given the crisis we are in?" the speaker asked, leaning into his microphone as the cameras rolled.

I could not say yes. I was not to apologize, nor could I apologize on behalf of the TLC. I didn't even work there. The mayor had taken an apology off the table, and I was told in my preparation that an apology could have legal consequences implicating the city in potential legal proceedings. So I simply stated that I did not know whether the current leadership should apologize and that I would work with the city council moving forward to alleviate suffering in the current crisis.

It was an answer, but it was not an authentic one.

One of the greatest lessons I learned from this experience was I needed freedom to speak authentically. I received a bit of guidance from a commissioner who had gone through the same process less than a year earlier. Her key bit of advice? Be authentic. She said that I would be given top-line speaking points that I should use when necessary but that I should speak from my authentic self.

I failed to do that. I kept to the rehearsed bullet points. I didn't speak from a position highlighting my own thoughts and opinions shaped by years of public service, including work with vulnerable populations. At the end of the day, I relied too much on the expertise of my guides through the process at the expense of listening to my inner voice.

You have to find a way to bring your own voice into the message. I could have done more of that, sharing my thoughts on some of the topics aside from the speaking notes. At the end of the day, you need both the space to say the high-level things you are required to say and some wiggle room to showcase your own thoughts and ideas.

LESSON #5: MENTAL BLOCKS HAPPEN

The council had also recently introduced a series of bills aimed at changing oversight of how the TLC regulated medallion transfers. "Do you have any thoughts about the bills we are considering and have introduced?" he asked.

That's where I drew a blank. I had read every bill related to the industry. I had taken notes and discussed them in detail, yet, in this moment when I was being grilled, I lost my footing. I couldn't think of the details, so I gave a superficial answer. He held his head in his hands and muttered that this was "awful." As he did, the cameras clicked, and I knew that was it. This would be the takeaway from this process. I remained calm, tried to showcase the top-line things I would do if confirmed, but I failed to engage as forcefully as required in the hearing.

My head cleared after the next question, and I interjected my thoughts about the specific bills, but it was too late. The damage had been done. The questions continued from other council members for another thirty minutes or so, but the tone and tenor of the hearing and my confirmation had already been determined.

Even with intense preparation, even if you *know* the answer to a question, mental blocks happen, and they can make or break a hearing. It's unfortunate, but that's life. All you can do is answer to the best of your ability and keep moving forward.

THE MOST IMPORTANT LESSON: LIFE GOES ON

Later that day and for the next several days, local news headlines played up that moment when the speaker held his head in his hands and called my performance "awful" and "terrible." They berated me for fumbling through the confirmation hearing, unable to provide any sense of an intelligible or coherent thought about what I would do if appointed. It sucked to read these things.

"City Council Driving Mayor de Blasio's Taxi Boss Nomination Off the Road" (Fisher 2019).

"Mayor de Blasio's Pick for Taxi Commission Gives 'Awful' Performance under Fire from City Council" (Sanders 2019).

"New York Needed a New Taxi Chief. But a Battle Got in the Way" (Rosenthal 2019b).

After the hearing, I traveled to far northern New York State to conduct training with my National Guard unit. I tried to keep abreast of the fallout via my phone, but it was tough. The mayor's team was strong in their defense of me the day following the hearing, but over the weekend and into Monday, the support seemed to wane in public statements. Then, finally, a few days after the hearing, the mayor's team let me know that they would withdraw my nomination while they determined how they were going to proceed.

"Mayor de Blasio Withdraws Taxi Commission Nominee Jeff Roth after Disastrous Council Hearing" (Braine 2019).

Not getting the job was rough, and it did not play out the way I wished it had. No one wants to be grilled publicly and come out looking as though they don't have any grasp of the issues. I am a believer, though, that things work out the way they are supposed to if not always how we want them to. My ego took a hit, but the message was very clear that I was not the person they wanted to head the agency.

Shortly after the hearing, a friend suggested that we grab lunch. He reminded me that people would not remember any of this a few weeks later and that I was now a player in NYC politics. He urged me to see the value in this moment even when things were rough.

The roller coaster of emotion that followed my nomination and the failed confirmation process was challenging, but some remarkable things had come from the experience. I had learned a lot from the process, and it was nothing I had ever had opportunity to do before. I'd had the opportunity to meet with the mayor one-on-one in Gracie Mansion. I'd received an outpouring of congratulation after I was formally nominated and prior to the confirmation hearing, and I'd met and worked with key leaders at city hall throughout the process. I got to know many of the public servants on that team with whom I had not worked in the past. I'd received phone calls from people in the taxi regulated industries congratulating me on the nomination and letting me know that they were looking forward to working with me.

I took a few licks, but life goes on. Remember, every time one door closes, another opens. You are not defined by your failures but by how you react to those failures. So when you make mistakes, even big ones, seek to learn from the experience, then look ahead for new opportunities and keep going.

KEY TAKEAWAYS

I learned a lot from this experience. There were a few key things that I should have demanded, and if ever put into a similar position, I will. I will make sure I have the opportunity to leverage my strengths and build one-on-one relationships, and I will make sure I have the freedom to be authentic.

My biggest regret is that I didn't get the opportunity to give my energy and attention to a serious crisis in which I could have made a difference...Oh, wait, not true. I did get that opportunity—a few months later and over 6,000 miles away. More on that in the next chapter.

CHAPTER 10

EMERGENCY MANAGEMENT

A crisis or disaster will hit and you will have to respond. Here are some lessons on how to respond to emergency situations.

"The fight is won or lost far away from witnesses—behind the lines, in the gym, and out there on the road, long before I dance under those lights."

—MUHAMMAD ALI

After the TLC position hadn't worked out, I called the leadership of my National Guard unit. "Do you have room for one more?" I asked the division's chief of staff, who had supported me throughout the confirmation process. His response was, "We sure do!" My National Guard unit was scheduled to deploy to the Middle East during the early part of 2020 for a ten-month rotation leading Task Force Spartan, which oversaw army training and exercises in several countries, including Egypt, Jordan, Kuwait, United Arab Emirates, and Saudi Arabia. The mission was to build relationships in that part of the world to protect the interests of the United States and its allies.

I had spent time in the region early in my army career as a first lieutenant when my unit was deployed to Sinai, Egypt. That earlier experience had been a phenomenal adventure and growth opportunity for me. Although I wasn't eager to be away from home for close to a year, I was ready for another opportunity to work with my guard unit, learn and grow professionally, and be part of something bigger than myself.

And I was off. After a series of training events that took us from Pennsylvania to Fort Hood, Texas, for several weeks, we boarded our flights to Kuwait. That was the location of the organization's headquarters, where I would be principally assigned. I was a field artillery officer, and my role and that of my team was to advise our senior commander on how various army and air force weapon systems could be leveraged to ensure the mission's success. This could be anything from key engagements with host nation leadership to conducting lethal rocket and missile fires in a combat situation. We always had to be prepared to do either or both.

A NEW MISSION

One morning early in the deployment, while I was working in my team's office area, the aide to our chief of staff walked in.

"I'm looking for Lieutenant Colonel Roth," she said to the members of my team, one of whom pointed down at me on the floor. "He's right there." I was on the floor doing a plank, a front hold that exercises the core muscles. It was plank day, and that's what we would do throughout the day.

"Oh, right. Sir, the chief of staff asked to see you."

I stood up, brushed myself off, and made my way over to his office.

"Sir, you wanted to see me?"

"Jeff, yes, have a seat," he said. "We've been tasked to establish a COVID-19 emergency operations center, and I want you to be its J3." A J3 is someone who serves as the chief of operations in a joint environment that includes personnel from more than one service branch.

This was before the novel coronavirus had reached alarming levels, and I had barely heard rumblings of the virus or pandemic. Oddly enough, though, during my graduate school experience, we had done a two-week exercise on pandemic preparation and response. Even though it had been several years earlier, it was a topic I had studied from a policy perspective.

Our chief of staff stepped over to his whiteboard to explain the situation in greater depth. He was always one to sketch a concept on the wall or paper to illustrate his thoughts on how to tackle a problem. In the discussion that followed, he outlined more of the problem statement. Essentially, we needed to stand up a cell that would be manned 24/7 from then until the end of the pandemic. We would monitor and track personnel who tested positive; establish quarantine and contact tracing policies; understand force health protection measures and best practices for mitigating the spread of the disease; manage the impacts of the pandemic on the travel of military personnel into and out of the countries we oversaw; and ensure we were abiding by all the host nations' requirements for quarantine of personnel traveling into or through our area. Additionally, we had to establish protocols to manage units that had or had not quarantined stateside, determine which installations had community spread or an outbreak, and mitigate that spread to our other personnel or installations.

We would oversee these operations across nearly thirty installations in six countries (Egypt, Jordan, Kuwait, Saudi Arabia, United Arab Emirates, and Qatar) with approximately 30,000 army service members, contractors, and civilians working throughout—and we had to have the cell up and running that day!

So there it was. My mission for the foreseeable future.

PLAN BEFORE THE CRISIS HITS

Muhammed Ali stated that the fight was won long before he stepped into the arena. Emergency response operations are the same. Having a plan in place and the relationships to manage it before the crisis hits is vital. No matter how imperfect it may be, a plan provides a starting point.

For the pandemic response, our higher headquarters already had a draft plan in place for that type of situation. My team's job was to build on and execute that plan.

I gathered my team and we set to work immediately, occupying a conference room across the hall from my office. It was small, but it had two computers, a whiteboard, and video-conferencing capability. Everything we needed. We scheduled a kickoff meeting for later that day with the stakeholders we could think of, and I met with our general officer and senior colonel to discuss how we would track these matters.[4] We pulled in our division's surgical cell and its medical service officers, who had already begun

---

4   General officers are the senior decision makers within the military, and our team reported to a brigadier general who was the officer in charge of our response efforts.

surveying, monitoring, and assessing the situation, and we began building relationships across all the various units throughout our area of operations to collectively protect our force.

Our days were very long, and we worked tirelessly to monitor and track conditions on the ground and establish policies and procedures across our area of operations. On top of managing the pandemic response, we were responsible for tracking the flow of forces into and out of Iraq and Afghanistan (Kuwait is a critical hub for that flow) for quarantine, quarantining soldiers arriving in the area who had not quarantined immediately prior to departure, building facilities to conduct these operations, monitoring medical evacuations, tracking the health of those who did become infected, and establishing conditions to reopen our installations once the threat was past.

Several tools and strategies helped us to succeed in these tasks, including predictive modeling, the use of a decision-support matrix, and routines.

MODELING MATTERS

Over the coming days, weeks, and even months, we tracked COVID-19 and our response across the entire area. We had our operations research and systems analysis officer conduct extensive modeling on when we expected each country's peak to occur and, if COVID-19 did break into an installation, how quickly it would spread and how much our mitigation measures would slow it. Our modeling predicted that we would hit our peak in mid- to late June at the earliest, with some assumptions putting us into mid- to late July.

The modeling mattered for a couple of reasons. We needed to know when each country would peak so that if one of our service members became infected and needed critical hospital care, we had some idea of when the host nation's medical facilities would be at capacity and unable to support us. If and when that time came, it would be crucial for us to evacuate any of our personnel who were sick out of the country before they deteriorated. We were learning from findings about the disease that decompensation could happen very quickly, particularly in older populations and those with preexisting medical conditions. Although the majority of our population consisted of service members, a fairly young and healthy group, we also had a number of contractors and civilians in our care who were older and had other health conditions.

A DECISION-SUPPORT MATRIX IS KEY

Knowing what actions to take in a sequence of events as certain conditions are met is key to managing a crisis. One of the best tools for this is a decision-support matrix, which lays out a conditions-based approach to making decisions. It's critical that you build a decision-support matrix *prior* to the crisis.

Our higher headquarters had produced a decision-support matrix that laid out various decisions that would be triggered as the disease reached pandemic levels. We printed it and hung it on the wall of our conference room along with all the other tracking materials that helped us paint a picture of conditions on the ground. It included the criteria that would raise us to various health protection condition levels (from A, normal operations, to D, which required sheltering in place and ceasing all operations). This became a checklist that we used to monitor the situation.

It also had the prescribed response mitigation measures that we would consider to protect the force in each health protection condition level. For example, in health condition level A, the threat of disease spread was very low and normal operations continued. However, that was the time to build and prepare quarantine and isolation facilities and stock them with equipment, identify our public health emergency officer, refine and rehearse medical evacuation procedures, and establish processes for reporting key information. Having the decision-support matrix meant that we didn't wait for the crisis to reach us but took measured steps to prepare.

The matrix also included the expected conditions on the ground in each location in the host country, such as the number of infections and the hospital capacity. In other words, it showed us what indicators to prioritize and information to collect to inform our response.

In addition to the key indicators of the decision-support matrix, we also established indicators that alerted us when an issue required intervention from higher level decision makers. That is, we had to respond when the status of certain resources (such as medical supplies or testing kits) reached certain levels.

As the pandemic developed and conditions worsened globally and locally, we monitored the key indicators that would alert us to when we should move into the next force health protection level and institute stricter response and mitigation measures. When we reached the identified indicators, we set in motion critical actions that would protect us if indeed the outbreak reached a pandemic.

When COVID-19 showed up on an installation, we established procedures for its commanders to declare a public health emergency (PHE) in accordance with Department of Defense instructions. The PHE gave the installation commander additional powers to respond and enforce mitigation measures. Declaring a PHE on the installation where I lived was invaluable to containing the spread, conducting contact tracing, and ensuring that everyone had performed an adequate quarantine in the continental United States before arrival or immediately upon arriving at our area of operations.

The decision-support matrix was critical to our ability to contain and manage the virus. It's valuable in any crisis. Think through a potential crisis that may affect you and your team. It doesn't have to be a global pandemic; it could be something like a negative press story about your project or program. Determine what conditions trigger a specific response, build a decision-support matrix, and use it to make decisions when your world becomes chaotic.

MAKE ROUTINE THINGS ROUTINE

Essential to managing a crisis is the process of making routine things routine; establishing the battle rhythm, reporting cycles, processes, and timelines for information pushes and pulls is critical.

Our team was small, but we established routines and battle tracking[5] that pulled and pushed information to the key stakeholders regularly and consistently. We had daily phone calls with our partner units to manage the flow of soldiers traveling through the area and to coor-

---

5 Battle tracking is the military's way of saying to track conditions on the ground or to monitor a situation as it develops.

dinate resources and medical supplies, and we created routines around tracking key information. We knew, for instance, that we needed to measure specific guideline criteria from the Centers for Disease Control and Prevention (such as the ability to test, treat, etc.) and our own capacity to isolate and quarantine personnel affected by the disease. We also had to know the threat level on each of our installations. We tracked the information of all the service members and their contacts in our area who were symptomatic and tested positive, who were put into quarantine.

Based on this information, we established routine reports that morphed as we refined them along the way. Starting with the critical items and building on that is the way to get started. Provide the data you know, work to collect what you need to know, and share it with your boss as you are able.

From a small conference room, in large part due to establishing routines, we were able to arm our commander with the key information necessary to enable his decision making and to support the protection of our troops.

Even with preparation, though, and a solid plan to guide and direct emergency response operations from the start, emergency situations are chaotic. At all steps along the way in our response, we encountered significant hurdles. The coronavirus was a new threat, and we were still learning about the disease and the impact it could have on a military population. There were a few examples of military installations where the virus had hit. However, early in the response, data were lacking about the infection rates and how many of those infected would need critical care. This uncertainty led to ambiguity in the face of the response and sometimes conflicting guidance or unclear instruction on how best to proceed as we dealt with daily challenges. The result was tension between the various senior leaders as we worked across organizations to coordinate responses. Focusing on painting the picture as best we could, though, as the situation unfolded was the best way we as an operations center could help our commander make decisions. Having a framework, even rudimentary, helped ease some of that tension in the face of the fog of the pandemic.

The coronavirus pandemic was my most recent foray into emergency management, but it was far from the first. Several times in my career I've been involved with managing crises, and each one has brought its own lessons. One of the most memorable was my experience with the Hurricane Sandy response in NYC.

REWIND EIGHT YEARS: HURRICANE SANDY ON THE HORIZON

It was late October and an absolutely beautiful weekend. The trees were in full autumn regalia with their splendid colors splashed across the rolling hills. It was Saturday evening, and we had just sat down to dinner, a formal affair with all attired in army dress blues. My National Guard unit was in Vermont for a training conference, joining leadership from across the division's units to look at training for the next several years and the path to deployment.[6] As the dinner wound down, a colleague of mine received a text message.

"I think this is going to be serious, and we will be activated," he said, glancing at his phone. He was on the distribution list for New York State National Guard alert messages. There had been chatter all weekend. Was Hurricane Sandy going to blow out to sea or come up the eastern seaboard and hit NYC? I was with my National Guard unit for the training weekend and was to travel home the next afternoon and return to my civilian life. Such is the routine of reservists and National Guard members from across the country who do this every month.

Later that evening, I learned that I would be returning to NYC but that I wouldn't go home. I would report to my armory. Before the dinner had ended, we knew the alert was going to come. We would stand up our battalion headquarters in Jamaica, Queens, the next night and marshal one hundred soldiers ready to support NYC as the storm

---

6   A division is a senior-level military organization with several brigades and battalions
    subordinate to it in its structure.

approached. We knew it was likely coming for us, and we would be ready to provide support to civil authorities such as police, fire, and emergency medical services.

The next morning, I drove home, packed my gear, and headed to the armory, where we stood up our operations center. I was the operations officer for the 400-soldier artillery battalion, responsible for overseeing all aspects of training and operations for the unit. A year earlier, the battalion had completed a rigorous training rotation at the National Training Center in Fort Irwin, California. Being tried in one of the army's combat readiness centers meant that we were tested. We were prepared for what the next days would bring us.

GOOD COMMUNICATION AND RELATIONSHIPS MAKE A DIFFERENCE

Interestingly, during this time, I was also an assistant commissioner of the FDNY. Having relationships that straddled both the military and the emergency response sector proved to be very valuable during our response operations. During the storm, there would be several support requests that required clarification. There was one incident in particular where the FDNY Queen's Borough Commander had requested high-axle military vehicles but wasn't clear for what use. Would a Humvee do or a larger truck of which we had a limited supply? The commander was someone I knew and worked with regularly at the FDNY. I called him on my cell and asked what he needed help with.

"Jeff, we need vehicles that can get down flooded streets to evacuate people," he said and explained how many he thought he needed. Having the ability to reach out and ask clarifying questions allowed us to respond with the right solution.

By that evening, we had assembled our soldiers at the armory and prepared for our missions. As the night fell, the rain and wind increased in ferocity. There was no letting up; Sandy was making her way up the seaboard, pushing surge waters into the Hudson River basin, overflowing flood zones. Our soldiers would deploy throughout the city to rescue those who needed help. I stood in the motor pool of our armory as we loaded our soldiers and supplies into vehicles, readying them to convoy into the night. They departed into the darkness where rainwaters and heavy winds were already devastating the city. We had a mission to complete and little idea of what we were headed into.

As Sandy approached NYC, the storm pushed water to fourteen-foot levels, flooding neighborhoods and homes, knocking out power and cell towers, and turning streets into unnavigable waterways. Our unit provided vehicles and personnel who supported rescue operations for the next several days. Our large trucks could go into neighborhoods where the water had flooded streets and ambulances were unable to go. We evacuated people in need and brought them to safety, where civil authorities could then provide care.

SIMPLIFY WITH A GO-SHEET

Throughout our response, I worked in our operations cell, coordinating our resources and matching requests for support to our available vehicles and soldiers. I reported to our battalion commander, who was constantly running between our units on the ground to assess what support they needed. He would then return to the operations cell for briefings and updates on personnel, equipment, and the status of our operations. He needed all the key information in a quick, easy-to-access format. Our solution was something we called the commander's go-sheet.

With the go-sheet, we devised a format that tracked a large quantity of information on a single page that our commander could put in his side pocket and take with him on the go. As he headed out the door each morning to assess the situation on the ground, we handed him the go-sheet, which included the status of his people, equipment, and vehicles, where they were located, and the missions they were supporting. Then, when he returned later in the day, we provided an updated go-sheet.

The go-sheet became a useful tool that allowed our battalion commander to quickly assess resources on hand, missions underway, and the location of people and assets. It included all the vital statistics he would need on a moment's notice to answer questions or provide data to our higher headquarters.

In a crisis, decision makers need reports that draw their attention to critical items, letting them quickly assess the situation and make decisions. So build a one-pager that your boss can take while on the go that provides in an organized way the high-level indicators and metrics that he or she can use in discussions and decision making. Use graphs and color coding to draw attention to the most important elements and where he or she should be focused.

DO A DAILY STORYBOARD OF HIGHLIGHTS

In emergency operations, days, weeks, and months become a blur. Remembering everything that occurred and when is challenging, so a daily digest or record of events becomes invaluable.

As the Hurricane Sandy emergency response continued, the days and weeks blended together. We were on autopilot, working ourselves to the bone. Some of our soldiers worked for days at a time, catching a few moments of rest in their Humvees when they could. The operations center operated nonstop to track our response. We paused only long enough to catch a couple of hours of sleep and kept going fueled by coffee and adrenaline.

Still, we took the time to document the emergency response as well as possible. At the end of each day, we did a storyboard of highlights from the day's operations. Our storyboards were built on a slide and included photos related to the mission we conducted and key highlights from the day, such as accomplishments, how many people we served, significant challenges, and so on. It was a way to tell our story and report to our higher headquarters everything that our unit had accomplished to help New Yorkers devastated by the storm. Having someone manage the history of the event and our actions ensured that we captured event details as they occurred, and it allowed us to reference the timeline as we went along.

One day in particular stands out. We were asked to distribute fuel to the local community, and a fuel truck was on its way to us from a military installation a couple of hours away. Word got out through social media that there was fuel available, and cars and people began lining up even before the fuel truck arrived. There were two pumps on the fuel truck, and one of them would not work. We then had to distribute the fuel using one pump handle even as thousands of people waited with empty containers to receive a gallon of fuel, the allotment for each person. This was one more day like many others on which we had to figure out the distribution of resources. During the crisis, you won't have time to process everything. Because we documented this event in a storyboard, after the event and the dust had settled, we could go back and review everything we had been through. With the fuel distribution, except for our storyboard, I would have forgotten how many gallons of gasoline we distributed, how many people had lined up to receive the fuel, and how we problem solved that day to complete the task at hand.

In an emergency, finding time to document key items every day is hard but critical. If you cannot do it, delegate someone to complete this task. Even a couple of sentences on what you faced on a given day will help you remember everything you did along the way and the key details that are too easy to forget in a crisis. It also helps you tell the story when all is said and done.

DO A PROJECT RECAP

At the end of our tour, we used our daily storyboards to create an overall project recap that showed how much we did to support our city when it was hard hit. We had saved lives and property. All our soldiers were New Yorkers, themselves affected by the storm, yet they worked tirelessly for days on end without showers, sleep, or hot meals.

During our emergency response operations, we conducted 170 search-and-rescue missions in Staten Island and the Rockaways; rescued and evacuated 800 people and 12 pets, including many elderly, disabled, or sick people from places such as nursing homes; respectfully recovered the remains of 8 people and returned them to their loving families; distributed 450,000 meals to 10 locations in Queens, Staten Island, Brooklyn, and Manhattan; delivered 35 mattresses and bed frames to a nursing home; exchanged 3 cell phone tower power cells; distributed 11,000 gallons of fuel to 571 cars and 844 people in Queens; provided 12,072 total man-hours focused on traffic control, presence patrols, house damage surveys, and tree and debris removal in partnership with the FDNY and NYPD through hurricane conditions and floodwaters as deep as four feet.

When I toured the city, I was awestruck. I remember crossing the bridge from Queens into Far Rockaway, an area of the city that had been particularly hard hit. Crossing the bridge and looking down at the waters that had receded, I saw just how high they had risen. Debris, including boats and cars, dotted the land, some of it in trees. Along the road into Far Rockaway, a peninsula that juts off from mainland Queens into the Atlantic Ocean, we saw cleanup crews from across the military branches and city agencies all working together to haul debris to collection points. Entire houses were moved, as if a giant hand had picked them up from their foundation and placed them down the street. They had stood no chance against the awesome power of the surge waters.

Amid all the destruction, though, was an incredible sense of community. There was work to be done. People came out of their homes, and neighbors helped neighbors to start the long, tedious process of rebuilding. I was proud to be part of it. Proud of the National Guard and the FDNY, members of both working together with other response organizations to take care of our families, neighborhoods, and city.

KEY TAKEAWAYS

Crisis operations are fast paced, exhausting, nonstop, and thrilling. Giving all your attention to an operation that quite literally protects human lives is meaningful.

For an effective emergency response, a crisis must be managed long before the crisis hits. In every massive emergency response operation, it is critical to be on the ground to assess the situation as best as possible (where conditions allow) and form policies and procedures to understand the conditions and how leadership should respond.

Developing methods for collecting information about the most critical items and tracking the development of a situation on a recurring basis are of the utmost importance. Use a decision-support matrix and routines to keep you on track.

Communication is also key. Develop relationships that allow for open communication, and learn to present critical information in a short, easy-to-use format, like a go-sheet.

Finally, make the time to document key items every day. Time is limited in an emergency, but documentation helps you improve processes and do a recap at the end of the process.

CONCLUSION

We stepped into the rickety basket and slowly descended into the hole that would take us 700 feet beneath Manhattan's bedrock—a view that not even the daily straphangers of NYC's subway system would ever see—into the drilling site of NYC's third water tunnel. It was my first week on the job as a policy analyst in the Mayor's Office of Operations under the leadership of Mayor Bloomberg. Little did I know that this basket ride would be the start of a twelve-year career working on some of the most complex and interesting policy questions vexing urban spaces. I would weave my way through a range of policy concentrations: flood mitigation, building demolition and public safety, risk mitigation, fire prediction modeling, small business economic development, emergency response, and taxi and Uber services. Then I would help build a brand-new city agency from initial idea to a fully functional organization.

My journey through NYC government was far different from anything I had experienced growing up at the back end of a dusty road in Milford, Michigan, a town of fewer than 7,000 people. As a teenager, I was introduced to the urban environment when I participated in a program offered by my high school that allowed me to visit inner-city Detroit one night each week to tutor youth in reading, math, and life skills. From there, I had opportunities to participate in humanitarian experiences in Mexico and Romania. Through these early life experiences, I became immersed in the harsh realities that existed all around me. I remember a conversation I had with twin brothers from Detroit. They were in tears because, as they put it, "Our daddy is in prison and our mother smokes too much pot." I also remember the thirteen-year-old boy I spent time with in Iași, Romania, who lived in a "house of children" and was forced to acknowledge on a daily basis the reality that his family had abandoned him. And I cannot forget the moment when, in a Romanian hospital for malnourished babies in the mid-1990s, I held a little girl in my arms who died only days later. These experiences opened my eyes to need and taught me that policy issues affect real people. As some of my earliest awakenings to troubling aspects of reality, they solidified my understanding of how public policies so clearly impact people's lives.

After earning a master's degree in public policy and urban planning, I was able to move to NYC, where I had the opportunity to yoke my policy interests to my urban planning skills and work on complex, ambiguous, and sometimes volatile urban policy issues that affected millions of people. I took away a renewed sense of the importance and impact of sound public policy, a deeper awareness of the role of our public institutions, and the conviction that we all have a duty as citizens to ensure the safety and protection of our public institutions.

Your story, though different, may share similar values. You are likely driven by a desire to make an impact, leave the world a little better than you found it, grapple in the messiness of public policy formation, or enjoy the thrill of serving political leaders who share your values. Whatever the motivation, you have a chance to be part of steering the ship, and you will find that bureaucracy is not always easily navigated, that creating change requires consistent, persistent effort. You will need two things. First, you need to know that you are not alone, that the work you do is part of our larger story, woven into the fabric of our public life. Realize that you are a steward of public resources and trust, do the best you can, and know that others like you are swimming upstream to make things a little better. Second, you must understand that the right tools, applied in the right ways, can help you more effectively achieve the results you need. Find those tools, refine them, and employ them to change the machinery of government, that unruly contraption, to become more efficient, more responsive, and more accountable to the people it was built to serve.

Whatever your passion, this guidebook was written to show how the lessons of the problems and projects I tackled can be applied in any situation. Understanding how to build project plans and recognizing the importance of organizing your team and people will achieve results. Spending the hours necessary to accurately size up the problem before identifying the solution will save time, energy, and precious public dollars. Learning from the expertise of others to guide your project or program is necessary for charting a path that gets you from point A to point B. As an analyst in any organization, you will have the opportunity to guide your boss or your stakeholders. Know where you want to take them and how you plan to get them there, and push them information all along the way.

Learning to weather the storms that come, both figuratively and literally, is crucial because they will undoubtedly come. In a crisis, distilling the most important elements for your boss and sharing them in a way that enables his or her quick decision making is as much art as science. Use the tools I offer here to present information in a way that is actionable and that answers the "So what?" question for your audience. Leverage data to create insight and focus decision-making energy where needed, when needed.

Finally, democracy requires participation from all citizens. Committing to the public sector is noble, demanding, and for those who want better, challenging. It is also intensely gratifying. It makes a difference, and you can feel it every day, particularly when working in local government, where operations have a direct, immediate impact on citizens' lives. We all have a duty to tackle big projects, to share with one another what we've learned along the way, and every day to justify the public's trust and confidence. If you've been drawn to read any of this book, that is what you, too, are called to do. Thank you for your service.

ACKNOWLEDGMENTS

Throughout this process, I have been guided by steady hands who know the business of writing books and supported my goal to share what I have learned in my public service with others. A special thank-you to my publisher, Natalie Aboudaoud, for keeping me on track and keeping this project on deadline. Your feedback and consistency carried it through. To the editing team, Kelsey Adams, Erin Sky, and Hal Clifford, thank you for bringing my words and ideas to life. You organized them in a way that I could not have possibly done myself, and have given shine to my roughhewn words. And the rest of the team, Rachael Brandenburg, Chas Hoppe, Miles Rote, Candace Sinclair, and Lisa Caskey, thank you for your feedback, guidance, and creativity. And to Carolyn Levin, thank you for the wise counsel.

Thank you to my weekly accountability team who encouraged me and pushed me when I needed it: Tom Gilman, Nick Gibbs, and Stan Prutz. You kept me focused on the goal. And a big thank you to Darren Hardy and the A-Team for pushing me forward.

A special thank-you to Alexis Wichowski for editing, coaching, and guiding me and my writing too many times to count.

Thank you to Shaquille Blake for always reminding me that the obstacle is the way, even when times feel tough.

Thank you to my team on deployment that continuously asked how I was progressing with my writing, and who made the deployment the amazing experience that it was: Chris Wallace, Adam Connolly, Vadim Yegorov, Ben Lewis, Oliver Sims, Real Richemard, Anthony Raco, Timothy Douglass, Austin Germadnik, Robert Vasquez Melendez, and Derrick Smith. And to my colleagues Jean Kratzer, Sean Murphy, and Trevor Cullen for providing me with that extra support.

To the dedicated public servants laboring in NYC government that I have had the distinct privilege to serve alongside. Your commitment to making an impact has inspired me, has made a difference in the lives of others, and has left the world better than you found it. There are too many people to name, but a few that I worked closely with who have guided me along the way:

The Mayor's Office of Operations team: Jeff Kay, Carole Post, Elizabeth Squadron, BJ Jones, Shana Whitehead, Amy Bishop, Alfredo Melian, Jeff Krupski, Emily Rubenstein, Jeanette Moy, Craig Hosang, and Kate Pielemeier.

The NYC Fire Department (FDNY): Sal Cassano, Don Shacknai, Michael Vecchi, Carolyn Kretz, Irene Sullivan, David Harney, Jeff Chen, Domenick Loccisano, Anthony Migliore, Chaz Thomas, Ryan Zirngibl, Darlene Hasselbring, Linda Shang, Malissa Smith, Chief Edward Kilduff, Chief Richard Tobin, Chief Joseph Pfeifer, Chief John Manahan, and Chief Abdo Nahmod.

My team and coworkers at the Taxi and Limousine Commission: Meera Joshi, Alan Fromberg, Chris Wilson, Midori Valdiva, Jo Rausen, Cindi Davidson, Rodney Stiles, Kala Wright, Justine Johnson, Dan Timmeny, Charles Furrey, Christon Charles, and the late Conan Freud. And to John Raskin of the Riders Alliance, with whom we worked closely for your leadership.

The Department of Veterans' Services: Loree Sutton, Jason Parker, Ellen Greeley, Nicole Branca, Venkat Motupalli, Eric Henry, Ines Adan, Latisha Russaw, Glenda Garcia, Gabe Ramos, Pedro Zapata, and Kwesi Douglas.

And finally, to those who bring special purpose to my life, my family and friends who have, by the examples of their own lives, taught me about service: Mom and Dad, Michael and Nicole Roth, Morgan Plummer, Kyle Marie Stock, Moe Vela, Michael Cairl, Juan Peña, Adrian Balestra, Luiza and Eric Pellerin, Cameron Burrell, and Jan Feuerstadt—you all serve and have served the causes you believe in. Thank you for your examples.

ABOUT THE AUTHOR

JEFF ROTH is an organizational leader who has served with distinction in both the public sector and the military. He was profiled in *Crain's New York Business*, which recognized Roth as a member of its "Class of 2014 Forty under Forty," its annual list of the most talented, driven, and dynamic professionals under the age of forty working in NYC. His work has appeared in *The Huffington Post, The New Republic,* and *USA Today. Fires, Floods, and Taxicabs: Taking a Bite Out of Big Apple Bureaucracy* is his first book and draws on his over twelve years of work in NYC government.

REFERENCES

Baker, Al. 2008. "Inquiry Lays Out Chain of Failures in High-Rise Fire." *The New York Times*, August 20. https://www.nytimes.com/2008/08/21/region/21deutsch.html?_r=1&adxnnl=1&oref=slogin&ref=nyregion&adxnnlx=1219339717-zns5lTejrJpHiybl98/fiw

Brain, Theresa. 2019. "Mayor de Blasio Withdraws Taxi Commission Nominee Jeff Roth after Disastrous Council Hearing." *New York Daily News*, July 22. https://www.nydailynews.com/news/politics/ny-taxi-commission-jeff-roth-nomination-withdrawn-de-blasio-20190722-yav4i4dprvfvlck2rlcxjolkwa-story.html.

Center for Active Design. Accessed September 6, 2020. https://centerforactivedesign.org/visionzero.

City of New York. 2008. *Strengthening the Safety, Oversight and Coordination of Construction, Demolition and Abatement Operations. Report and Recommendations to Mayor Michael R. Bloomberg.* New York: City of New York.

City of New York. 2014. *Vision Zero Action Plan.* New York: City of New York.

City of New York. 2020a. *Mayor's Management Report Preliminary Fiscal 2020*. New York: Mayor's Office of Operations.

City of New York. 2020b. *Vision Zero Year 6 Report*. New York: City of New York.

Dalio, Ray. 2017. *Principles: Life and Work*. New York: Simon & Schuster.

Davenport, Thomas H., and Jeanne G. Harris. 2017. *Competing on Analytics: The New Science of Winning*. Boston: Harvard Business School.

Durkin, Erin. 2015. "NYC to Launch New Department of Veterans' Services to Help City Vets Find Housing, Jobs, and Medical Care." *New York Daily News*, November 11. https://www.nydailynews.com/new-york/nyc-launch-new-department-veterans-services-article-1.2430284.

Dwoskin, Elizabeth. 2014. "How New York's Fire Department Uses Data Mining." *Wall Street Journal*, January 24. https://blogs.wsj.com/digits/2014/01/24/how-new-yorks-fire-department-uses-data-mining/.

Feuer, Alan. 2013. "The Mayor's Geek Squad." *The New York Times*, March 23. https://archive.nytimes.com/www.nytimes.com/2013/03/24/nyregion/mayor-bloombergs-geek-squad.html.

Fisher, Janon. 2019. "City Council Driving Mayor de Blasio's Taxi Boss Nomination off the Road." *New York Daily News*, July 19. https://www.nydailynews.com/news/politics/ny-jeff-roth-ritchie-torres-taxi-and-limousine-commission-nomination-20190719-f37qzzaxhve630wr2wllmch52m-story.html.

Fitzsimmons, Emma G. 2018. "Why Are Taxi Drivers in New York Killing Themselves?" *The New York Times*, December 2. https://www.nytimes.com/2018/12/02/nyregion/taxi-drivers-suicide-nyc.html#~:text=A%20taxi%20driver%20named%20Roy,the%20deaths%20as%20an%20epidemic.

Horowitz, Ben. 2014. *The Hard Thing about Hard Things: Building a Business When There Are No Easy Answers*. New York: Harper Collins.

Kosoff, Maya. 2015. "Uber Has a Clever Response to a Proposed Law that Could Kneecap the Company in One of Its Largest Markets." *Business Insider*, July 16. https://www.businessinsider.com/why-uber-has-a-de-blasio-car-option-in-new-york-city-2015-7.

Kugler, Sara. 2007. "Citing Lapses in Deutsche Bank Fire, N.Y. City Orders Building Inspections." *Insurance Journal*, August 29. https://www.insurancejournal.com/news/east/2007/08/29/83070.htm.

McChesney, Chris, Sean Covey, and Jim Huling. 2012. *The 4 Disciplines of Execution: Achieving Your Wildly Important Goals*. New York: Simon & Schuster.

McEnery, Thornton. 2014. "Crain's New York Business 40 under 40 Jeffrey Roth, 35." *Crain's New York Business*, April. https://www.crainsnewyork.com/awards/jeffrey-roth-35.

New York City Taxi and Limousine Commission. 2014. *Notice of Promulgation of Rules*. New York: New York City Taxi and Limousine Commission. https://www1.nyc.gov/assets/tlc/downloads/pdf/newly_passed_rules_fhv_dispatch_rules.pdf.

New York City Taxi and Limousine Commission. 2015. "Drive like Your Family Lives Here." New York City Taxi and Limousine Commission, March 30. YouTube video. https://www.youtube.com/watch?v=OAnSw3nzjoU.

Nonko, Emily. 2019. "What Does the Future Hold for NYC's Vision Zero Plan?" *Curbed New York*, August 19. https://ny.curbed.com/2019/8/19/20812166/new-york-city-vision-zero-bike-street-safety.

NYC Fire Wire. 2016. "Deutsche Bank Fire." *NYC Fire Wire*, August 18. https://nycfirewire.net/news/entry/deutsche-bank-fire.

Office of the Mayor. 2009. "Mayor Bloomberg Unveils Connected City Initiative." NYC.gov, October 1. https://www1.nyc.gov/office-of-the-mayor/news/432-09/mayor-bloomberg-connected-city-initiative.

Pazmino, Gloria. 2016. "After Long Process, City Launches New Department of Veterans' Services." *Politico*, April 8. https://www.politico.com/states/new-york/city-hall/story/2016/04/after-long-process-city-launches-new-department-of-veterans-services-033252.

Ries, Eric. 2011. *The Lean Startup*. New York: Crown.

Rivera, Ray. 2007. "2 Firefighters Are Dead in Deutsche Bank Fire." *The New York Times City Room*, August 18. https://cityroom.blogs.nytimes.com/2007/08/18/2-firefighters-are-dead-in-deutsche-bank-fire/

Rivera, Ray, and Fernanda Santos. 2007. "2 Firefighters Are Killed in Blaze at Ground Zero." *The New York Times*, August 19. https://www.nytimes.com/2007/08/19/nyregion/19fire.html.

Roman, Jesse. 2014. "In Pursuit of Smart." *NFPA Journal*, November/December, 41–50.

Rosenthal, Brian M. 2019a. "A Bailout for Taxi Drivers? The Mayor Says No, but Others Keep Pushing." *The New York Times*, July 8. https://www.nytimes.com/2019/07/08/nyregion/nyc-taxi-medallion-bailout.html.

Rosenthal, Brian M. 2019b. "New York Needed a Taxi Chief but a Battle Got in the Way." *The New York Times*, July 23. https://www.nytimes.com/2019/07/23/nyregion/bill-de-blasio-taxi-commissioner.html.

Sanders, Anna. 2019. "Mayor de Blasio's Pick for Taxi Commission Gives 'Awful' Performance under Fire from City Council." *New York Daily News*, July 18. https://www.nydailynews.com/news/politics/ny-council-mayor-de-blasio-jeff-roth-taxi-limousine-commission-tlc-20190718-4iqenw3a3veoxfdycvy6j2cwpu-story.html.

Shulzberger, A. G. 2009. "Reaching 311, via New iPhone App." *The New York Times*, October 1. https://cityroom.blogs.nytimes.com/2009/10/01/reaching-311-via-new-iphone-app/.

Tepper, Fitz. 2015. "Uber Launches 'De Blasio's Uber' Feature in NYC with 25-Minute Wait Times." *Tech Crunch*, July 17. https://techcrunch.com/2015/07/16/uber-launches-de-blasios-uber-feature-in-nyc-with-25-minute-wait-times/.

Urban Omnibus. 2009. "The Omnibus Roundup—Smarter Cities, Phantom Cities, Green Cities." *Urban Omnibus*, October 2. https://urbanomnibus.net/2009/10/the-omnibus-roundup-20/.

Made in the USA
Las Vegas, NV
09 March 2021

19292675R10163